modern neutrals

A FRESH LOOK AT NEUTRAL QUILT PATTERNS

AMY ELLIS

Martingale®
Create with Confidence

DEDICATION

To my husband, Joe, who is my constant support,
and a great sounding board for all my quilty ideas.

Modern Neutrals:
A Fresh Look at Neutral Quilt Patterns
© 2013 by Amy Ellis

Martingale®
19021 120th Ave. NE, Ste. 102
Bothell, WA 98011-9511 USA
ShopMartingale.com

Printed in China
18 17 16 15   8 7 6 5 4 3 2

Library of Congress Cataloging-in-Publication Data is
available upon request.

ISBN: 978-1-60468-323-3

Mission Statement
Dedicated to providing quality products
and service to inspire creativity.

CREDITS
President & CEO: Tom Wierzbicki
Editor in Chief: Mary V. Green
Design Director: Paula Schlosser
Managing Editor: Karen Costello Soltys
Acquisitions Editor: Karen M. Burns
Technical Editor: Nancy Mahoney
Copy Editor: Tiffany Mottet
Production Manager: Regina Girard
Cover & Text Designer: Adrienne Smitke
Illustrator: Lisa Lauch
Photographer: Brent Kane

contents

introduction

The inspiration for this book came when I realized that not everyone loves a bold, vibrant pattern as much as I do. This book is for those who want their quilts to accent and accompany modern living spaces. Layering texture and fabrics is the cornerstone of beautifully designed rooms. Read "Neutral Fabrics in Your Neutral Spaces," opposite, for my advice on working with neutrals before you begin.

Another source of inspiration was my husband. Joe has been a constant source of encouragement for my quilting passion. Until I wrote this book, however, he was the only one in our family without a quilt specifically pieced for him. Either my block design was too fussy or the fabric choices were too bold, so I was inspired to create patterns with colors he would appreciate. I'm certain there are family members and friends in your life you could say the same about, and I'm happy to offer an alternative source of ideas.

I hope you find these graphic, modern quilt patterns exciting, and that they help you start your next project.

~ Amy

neutral fabrics in your neutral spaces

Carefully thought-out and layered neutral spaces have a depth of interest beyond the paint color on the walls or the splash of color in an area rug. Adding an additional layer of interest in the form of a quilt will personalize your space with your unique creative voice.

Before selecting fabric for your quilt, step back and take a look at your room. What are the color variations in your space? Are they warm, cool, light, or dark? Is there a shade that is missing? Perhaps you want to add a bit of warmth to a gray room. Or, maybe the opposite is true, such as a cream room needing a modern touch of gray. Perhaps you're renting your space and white walls are what you have to work with. What textures are present in the room? Are they hard, soft, rough, or smooth? Understanding what is already present in your space will help in selecting fabrics, essentially filling in any gaps that you might have in your room.

When I started looking for fabrics to include in my neutral quilts, I was impressed with how many neutral fabrics I already had in my small stash. They've been used to create contrast in my previous quilts. However, I'm now creating contrast in texture and variation of color. Noticing subtle differences in color in a neutral palette is exciting and lends itself to inspired quilts. If

your project requires contrast, look to include midrange and deep tones, or use warm and cool tones to achieve the effect.

Neutral fabrics vary hugely in spectrum—from lightest ivory to deep chocolate brown, or bright white to soft black. You'll find more and more neutral fabrics as you create with them. Does your space need a light and airy palette? Or possibly a quilt of medium tones? I'm of the mind that it is acceptable to mix beige and gray palettes as you pull out fabrics; simply try to keep things harmonious.

Solid fabrics are a natural first step in a neutral quilt, but I urge you not to stop there. When I add prints to my quilts, the quilts seem to sparkle and have even more texture. Also, consider looking for linen or silk fabrics to include in your quilt. The color of these fabrics may be very similar to cotton fabrics, but the contrast in texture (smooth, shiny, or rough) will add depth to your quilt.

Once you've decided on a project and you're ready to begin, select fabrics for your project and lay them out together. Whether you're looking at your stash or in a store, your process should be the same. Looking at the group of fabrics, are there any that stand out? Usually, those fabrics have too much contrast for your project, or they are simply the wrong color. If you remove that one fabric, does the group feel more comfortable together? If you find one fabric that you love and want to base the quilt around, make sure it fits in your chosen color scheme and will read as a neutral in your quilt.

To aid in the fabric-selection process, I've labeled the fabrics A to D, with A being the lightest in the collection, and D being the darkest. Fabrics B and C are your medium tones, which can often be quite similar in color and value, but a little differentiation will be necessary depending on your project (see "Pivot" on page 15). As you're gathering fabrics for your next project, think about fabric value, and classify each as A through D. If you're looking only for A and C fabrics, you can eliminate the B and D fabrics as you gather. I also use prints from an array of fabric collections; this results in more variety within the quilt top and gives you options while shopping for (or in) your stash. If you buy one-yard cuts of your favorite neutrals, you'll have a great collection to work with whenever you're ready to start a new project.

Include small-scale geometric, floral, text, and polka-dot prints in your quilts and stash. In some cases, large-scale floral prints will also work, but I have not found many that are neutral in tone—stock up on those when you find them. Usually the fabric designer is inclined to add generous pops of color to large-scale floral prints. Neutral batik and hand-dyed fabrics are a nice addition; both of these options often include subtle variations in tone and add interest to quilts.

With these concepts in mind, the projects in this book are meant to inspire and encourage you to quilt with your own creative voice. Enjoying the process is just as important as the beautiful quilt you create. So have fun!

Examples of fabrics used in this book

Designed and pieced by Amy Ellis; machine quilted by Natalia Bonner

pleated patchwork

FINISHED QUILT: 60½" x 70½"
FINISHED BLOCK: 10" x 10"

"Pleated Patchwork" is the perfect introduction to working with neutrals. Look in your stash for a variety of prints and solids to use; if you haven't started collecting solids yet, you may be surprised by how many are already in your stash. The texture of the pleats adds depth and a nice cozy weight to your quilt.

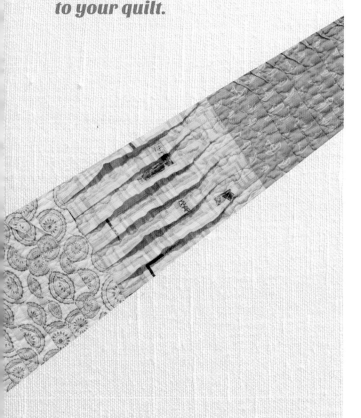

MATERIALS

Yardage is based on 42"-wide fabric.

42 rectangles, 10½" x 18", of assorted A and B
    fabrics (lightest and medium) for blocks
¾ yard of fabric for binding
4⅜ yards of fabric for backing
66" x 76" piece of batting
Water-soluble marker
Fabric glue stick

CUTTING

From the binding fabric, cut:
8 strips, 2½" x 42"

MAKING THE BLOCKS

Marking fold lines makes quick work of these pleated blocks. Work on a flat surface to make sure that the lines are straight.

1. On the right side of each rectangle, measure 9" from the short end as shown and use a water-soluble marker to draw a center line. Measure 2" from the center line and draw another line. Continue marking lines 2" apart, in both directions, until you have seven lines total.

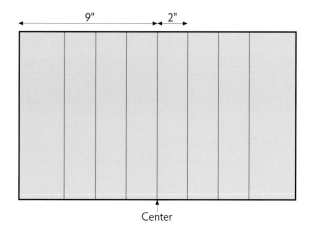

Center

2. On one end of a marked rectangle, fold along the first line, wrong sides together, and finger-press. Sew ½" from the folded edge to make a pleat.

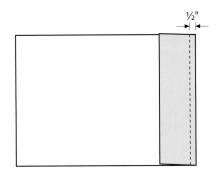

3. Repeat step 2, sewing a pleat at each marked line until you have seven pleats. Press the pleats to one side, gently tugging along each pleat to avoid additional folds. Trim the block to 10½" x 10½". Make 42 blocks.

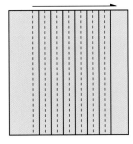

Make 42.

4. Along one pleated edge on each block, machine baste the pleats ⅛" from the raw edge or use a fabric glue stick to secure the pleats, making sure all the pleats are going in the same direction. On the opposite edge, flip the pleats in the other direction as shown in the photo on page 6 and baste or glue in place.

ASSEMBLING THE QUILT TOP

1. Lay out seven rows of six blocks each, rotating the blocks as shown. Pin and sew the blocks together in rows, pressing the seam allowances in opposite directions from row to row.

2. Pin and sew the rows together to complete the quilt top. Press the seam allowances in one direction.

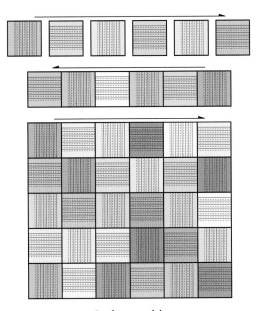

Quilt assembly

FINISHING THE QUILT

1. Cut the length of the backing fabric in half to create two 78"-long pieces. Sew the two pieces together side by side and press the seam allowances open.

2. Referring to "Basting a Quilt Sandwich" on page 77, layer the backing, batting, and quilt top; then baste the layers together. Use your favorite quilting technique to quilt a design that you love. In this quilt, Natalia quilted a wavy line between each pleat.

3. Referring to "Binding" on page 78 and using the 2½"-wide strips, bind your quilt.

circuit board

FINISHED QUILT: 72½" x 96½"
FINISHED BLOCK: 12" x 12"

"Circuit Board" is a very engaging quilt. Nine-patch units anchor the block corners, creating a box, and then the block is divided diagonally through the center. Alternating the blocks in value and rotating them makes for fantastic results with tons of interest!

MATERIALS

Yardage is based on 42"-wide fabric.

4¼ yards *total* of assorted A fabrics (lightest) for blocks

2¾ yards *total* of assorted B fabrics (medium) for blocks

2¾ yards *total* of assorted C fabrics (medium) for blocks

¾ yard of fabric for binding

6 yards of fabric for backing

78" x 102" piece of batting

> ### Throw Quilt Option
>
> To make 30 blocks for a quilt measuring 60½" x 72½", you'll need:
>
> 2⅔ yards *total* of assorted A fabrics (lightest) for blocks
>
> 1⅞ yards *total* of assorted B fabrics (medium) for blocks
>
> 1⅞ yards *total* of assorted C fabrics (medium) for blocks
>
> ⅝ yard of fabric for binding
>
> 4 yards of fabric for backing
>
> 66" x 78" piece of batting

Continued on page 11

Designed by Amy Ellis; pieced by April Rosenthal; machine quilted by Natalia Bonner

CUTTING

From the assorted A fabrics, cut *a total of:*
24 strips, 4½" x 42"; crosscut into 192 squares,
  4½" x 4½"
6 strips, 2½" x 42"; crosscut into 96 squares,
  2½" x 2½"
8 strips, 1½" x 42"

From the assorted B fabrics, cut *a total of:*
13 strips, 4½" x 42"; crosscut into:
  24 squares, 4½" x 4½"
  192 rectangles, 2" x 4½"
8 strips, 2" x 42"
6 strips, 2½" x 42"; crosscut into 96 squares,
  2½" x 2½"

From the assorted C fabrics, cut *a total of:*
13 strips, 4½" x 42"; crosscut into:
  24 squares, 4½" x 4½"
  192 rectangles, 2" x 4½"
8 strips, 2" x 42"
6 strips, 2½" x 42"; crosscut into 96 squares,
  2½" x 2½"

From the binding fabric, cut:
9 strips, 2½" x 42"

PIECING THE BLOCKS

1. Sew matching 2"-wide B or C strips to both
long sides of a 1½"-wide A strip. Press the
seam allowances outward. Make four strip
sets of each color combination (eight total).
Cut 96 B segments and 96 C segments,
1½" wide.

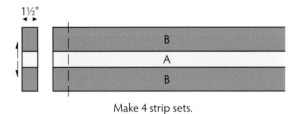

Make 4 strip sets.
Cut 96 segments.

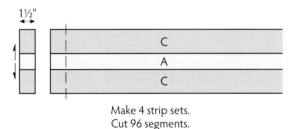

Make 4 strip sets.
Cut 96 segments.

2. Sew matching 2" x 4½" rectangles to the top
and bottom of each pieced segment. Press
the seam allowances outward. Make 96 B
units and 96 C units.

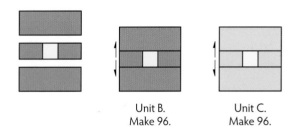

Unit B.
Make 96.

Unit C.
Make 96.

3. Mark a diagonal line on the wrong side of *all*
of the 2½" squares.

4. Matching the corners, pin a 2½" B square to a 4½" A square. Sew on the marked line. Trim the excess corner fabric ¼" from the stitched line. Press the seam allowances toward the resulting triangle. Repeat to make 96 units with B corners. In the same manner, sew the 2½" C squares to the remaining 4½" A squares to make 96 units with C corners.

Make 96 with B corners.
Make 96 with C corners.

5. Matching the corners, pin 2½" A squares to opposite corners of the 4½" B and C squares as shown. Sew on the marked line. Trim the excess corner fabric ¼" from the stitched line. Press the seam allowances toward the resulting triangles. Make 24 of each.

Make 24 with B squares.
Make 24 with C squares.

6. Lay out the block units in two rows as shown, making sure to differentiate between the B and C units. Join the units into rows and press the seam allowances in the direction indicated.

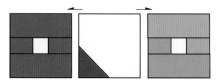

Row A.
Make 48 with B units and 48 with C units.

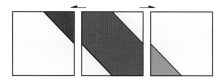

Row B.
Make 24 with B units and 24 with C units.

7. Sew two A rows and one B row together to complete a block. Press the seam allowances outward. Make 24 blocks with B units and 24 blocks with C units (48 total).

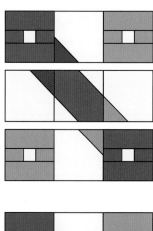

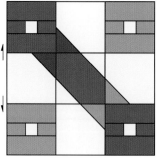

Make 48.

ASSEMBLING THE QUILT TOP

1. Lay out eight rows of six blocks each, alternating the blocks and rotating them as shown in the quilt assembly diagram below. Pin and sew the blocks together in rows, pressing the seam allowances in opposite directions from row to row.
2. Sew the rows together to complete the quilt top. Press the seam allowances in one direction.

FINISHING THE QUILT

1. Cut the length of the backing fabric in half to create two 108"-long pieces. Sew the two pieces together side by side and press the seam allowances open.
2. Referring to "Basting a Quilt Sandwich" on page 77, layer the backing, batting, and quilt top; then baste the layers together. Use your favorite quilting technique to quilt a design that you love.
3. Referring to "Binding" on page 78 and using the 2½"-wide strips, bind your quilt.

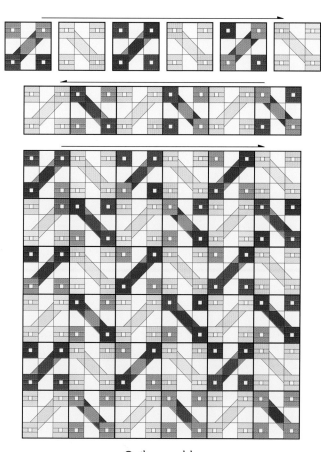

Quilt assembly

Designed and pieced by Amy Ellis; machine quilted by Natalia Bonner

pivot

"Pivot" is a great skill builder. Using pins as you piece will ensure that your bias edges aren't stretched, and a little starch helps too. The dynamic shapes might be overwhelmed by some fabric choices, so take careful notice of fabric tones to achieve the best results.

FINISHED QUILT: 54½" x 63½"
FINISHED BLOCK: 9" x 9"

MATERIALS

Yardage is based on 42"-wide fabric.

1⅓ yards of A fabric (lightest) for blocks
1⅛ yards *each* of 2 B fabrics (medium) for blocks
1⅓ yards of C fabric (medium) for blocks
⅝ yard of fabric for binding
3½ yards of fabric for backing
60" x 69" piece of batting

CUTTING

From *each* of the A and C fabrics, cut:
6 strips, 4¾" x 42"; crosscut into 42 squares, 4¾" x 4¾" (84 total)
3 strips, 3⅞" x 42"; crosscut into 21 squares, 3⅞" x 3⅞" (42 total). Cut the squares in half diagonally to yield 84 triangles.*

From *each* of the B fabrics, cut:
5 strips, 3⅞" x 42"; crosscut into 42 squares, 3⅞" x 3⅞" (84 total). Cut the squares in half diagonally to yield 168 triangles.*
4 strips, 3½" x 42"; crosscut into 42 squares, 3½" x 3½" (84 total)

From the binding fabric, cut:
7 strips, 2½" x 42"

*If you're using a GO! cutter, don't cut these pieces. See "Ready, Set, GO!" on page 16 instead.

PIECING THE BLOCKS

While this block looks complicated, piecing it in thirds eliminates any inset seams, and makes for quick construction.

1. Sew the C triangles to the A squares. Sew the A triangles to the C squares. Press the seam allowances toward the C fabric. Make 42 of each unit.

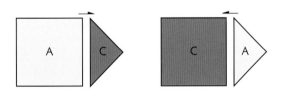

Make 42 of each.

2. Sew the units from step 1 together in pairs as shown. Press the seam allowances toward the C fabric. Make 42 block centers.

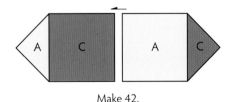

Make 42.

3. Matching the edges as shown, sew a B triangle to a B square, making sure to combine different B fabrics. Press the seam allowances toward the square. Make 42 of each unit.

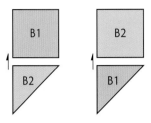

Make 42 of each.

4. Sew a matching triangle to the adjacent side of each unit from step 3 to make a pieced triangle unit. Press the seam allowances toward the triangle. Make 42 of each unit.

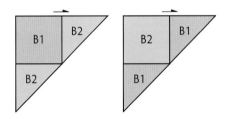

Make 42 of each.

5. Pin and sew the pieced triangle units to opposite sides of each center unit as shown to complete the blocks. Press the seam allowances in one direction. Make 42 blocks.

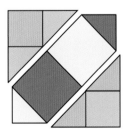
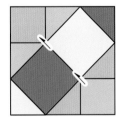

Make 42.

ASSEMBLING THE QUILT TOP

1. Lay out seven rows of six blocks each, rotating the blocks as shown in the quilt assembly diagram below. Pin and sew the blocks together in rows, pressing the seam allowances in opposite directions from row to row.

2. Sew the rows together to complete the quilt top. Press the seam allowances in one direction.

FINISHING THE QUILT

1. Cut the length of the backing fabric in half to create two 60"-long pieces. Sew the two pieces together side by side and press the seam allowances open.

2. Referring to "Basting a Quilt Sandwich" on page 77, layer the backing, batting, and quilt top; then baste the layers together. Use your favorite quilting technique to quilt a design that you love.

3. Referring to "Binding" on page 78 and using the 2½"-wide strips, bind your quilt.

Quilt assembly

Designed by Amy Ellis; pieced by Amy Smart; machine quilted by Natalia Bonner

waves

FINISHED QUILT: 60½" x 72½"
FINISHED BLOCK: 12" x 12"

The graphic design of "Waves" is an eye-catcher! Putting simple techniques to use, this quilt will be a favorite to make and give. Consider using only A and B fabrics for a lighter, more airy quilt; or use only A and D fabrics to highlight the graphic design.

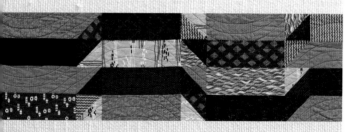

MATERIALS

Yardage is based on 42"-wide fabric.

2½ yards *total* of assorted C fabrics (medium) for blocks
2½ yards *total* of assorted D fabrics (darkest) for blocks
⅝ yard of fabric for binding
4 yards of fabric for backing
66" x 78" piece of batting

CUTTING

From the assorted C fabrics, cut *a total of:*
3 strips, 8" x 42"; crosscut into 15 squares, 8" x 8"*
16 strips, 3½" x 42"

From the assorted D fabrics, cut *a total of:*
3 strips, 8" x 42"; crosscut into 15 squares, 8" x 8"*
16 strips, 3½" x 42"

From the binding fabric, cut:
7 strips, 2½" x 42"

*If you're using a GO! cutter, don't cut these pieces. See "Ready, Set, GO!" below instead.

> **Ready, Set, GO!**
> If you have a GO! cutter and the 3"-finished half-square-triangle die, you may choose to assemble the half-square-triangle units from die-cut pieces. Cut six strips, 4" wide, from each of the C and D fabrics in place of the 8"-wide strips in the cutting instructions. Fold each strip into five layers before running it through the GO! cutter, yielding 120 triangles of each color.

PIECING THE BLOCKS

1. To make half-square-triangle units, draw intersecting diagonal lines on the wrong side of each 8" C square. Layer each marked square with a D square, right sides together. Sew ¼" on each side of both drawn lines.

 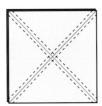

2. Cut the squares apart horizontally and vertically. Then cut the squares on the drawn diagonal lines to make 120 half-square-triangle units. Press the seam allowances toward the D fabric. Trim the units to measure 3½" square.

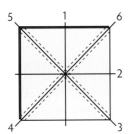

Make 120.

Half-Square-Triangle Trimming

I find I achieve better results when I make half-square-triangle units slightly bigger than necessary. This way I can trim them to the exact size I need. To trim the units, use a small square ruler with a 45° line. Align the 45° line on the ruler with the seam line and trim two sides of the unit. Rotate the unit and trim the other two sides. While sometimes tedious, this step makes block assembly a breeze and lost triangle points a thing of the past.

3. Sew a C strip to a D strip to make a strip set. Press the seam allowances toward the D strip. Make 16 strip sets.

Make 16.

4. Join two different strip sets from step 3, alternating the C and D strips as shown. Press the seam allowances in the same direction as the other seam allowances. Make eight strip sets. Cut the strip sets into 30 segments, 9½" wide.

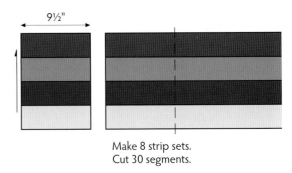

Make 8 strip sets.
Cut 30 segments.

5. Sew four half-square-triangle units together as shown. Press the seam allowances in the direction indicated by the arrows to create opposing seams.

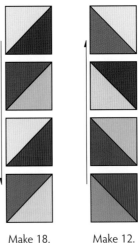

Make 18.   Make 12.

6. Using the 18 units from step 5, pin and sew each unit to a segment from step 4 as shown to make block A. Make 18 blocks, pressing the seam allowances in opposite directions from block to block.

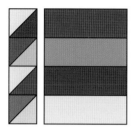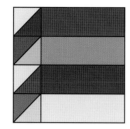

Block A.
Make 18.

7. Using the 12 units from step 5, pin and sew each unit to a segment from step 4 as shown to make block B. Make 12 blocks, pressing the seam allowances in opposite directions from block to block.

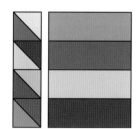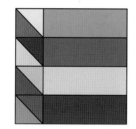

Block B.
Make 12.

ASSEMBLING THE QUILT TOP

1. Beginning and ending with an A block, lay out six rows of five blocks each, alternating the A and B blocks in each row, as shown in the quilt assembly diagram at right. Pin and sew the blocks together in rows, pressing the seam allowances in opposite directions from row to row.

2. Pin and sew the rows together to complete the quilt top. Press the seam allowances in one direction.

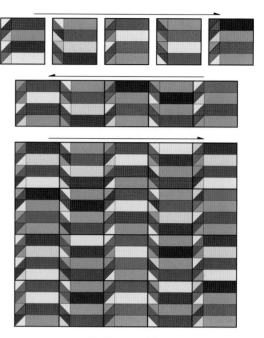

Quilt assembly

FINISHING THE QUILT

1. Cut the length of the backing fabric in half to create two 72"-long pieces. Sew the two pieces together side by side and press the seam allowances open.

2. Referring to "Basting a Quilt Sandwich" on page 77, layer the backing, batting, and quilt top; then baste the layers together. Use your favorite quilting technique to quilt a design that you love.

3. Referring to "Binding" on page 78 and using the 2½"-wide strips, bind your quilt.

Designed and pieced by Amy Ellis; machine quilted by Natalia Bonner

sliced

FINISHED QUILT: 54½" x 54½"
FINISHED BLOCK: 9½" x 9½"

"Sliced" is a fun quilt to make. The blocks are cut and sewn back together to make unique mirrored blocks. Setting the blocks on point brings the diagonal cuts back to the vertical, making the quilt quite intriguing. Position the blocks carefully in each diagonal half of the quilt top to complete the look.

MATERIALS

Yardage is based on 42"-wide fabric.

⅝ yard *each* of D3 and D4 fabrics (darkest) for blocks*
⅞ yard of A1 fabric (lightest) for blocks*
¾ yard of A2 fabric (lightest) for blocks*
¾ yard of D1 fabric (darkest) for blocks*
⅝ yard of A3 fabric (lightest) for blocks*
⅓ yard of D2 fabric (darkest) for blocks*
1⅛ yards *each* of 2 fabrics (1 light and 1 dark) for binding
2¾ yards of fabric for backing**
60" x 60" piece of batting

If you prefer a less scrappy quilt, you'll need 2¼ yards each of fabrics A and D.

**You'll need 3½ yards if you don't want an additional seam in your backing.*

CUTTING

From the A1 fabric, cut:
1 strip, 14⅝" x 42"; crosscut into 2 squares, 14⅝" x 14⅝". Cut the squares into quarters diagonally to yield 8 triangles.
6 strips, 2" x 42"; crosscut into:
    6 rectangles, 2" x 10½"
    12 rectangles, 2" x 9"
    6 rectangles, 2" x 7½"
3 squares, 4" x 4"

From the A2 fabric, cut:
1 strip, 4" x 42"; crosscut into 6 squares, 4" x 4"
4 strips, 3" x 42"; crosscut into:
    12 rectangles, 3" x 6½"
    12 rectangles, 3" x 5"
4 strips, 1½" x 42"; crosscut into:
    12 rectangles, 1½" x 7½"
    12 rectangles, 1½" x 4"

Continued on page 24

From the A3 fabric, cut:

6 strips, 2" x 42"; crosscut into:
    6 rectangles, 2" x 10½"
    12 rectangles, 2" x 9"
    6 rectangles, 2" x 7½"
3 squares, 4" x 4"

From the D1 fabric, cut:

1 strip, 14⅝" x 42"; crosscut into 2 squares,
    14⅝" x 14⅝". Cut the squares into quarters
    diagonally to yield 8 triangles.
4 strips, 2" x 42"; crosscut into:
    4 rectangles, 2" x 10½"
    8 rectangles, 2" x 9"
    4 rectangles, 2" x 7½"
6 squares, 4" x 4"

From the D2 fabric, cut:

2 strips, 3" x 42"; crosscut into:
    6 rectangles, 3" x 6½"
    6 rectangles, 3" x 5"
2 strips, 1½" x 42"; crosscut into:
    6 rectangles, 1½" x 7½"
    6 rectangles, 1½" x 4"

From *each* of the D3 and D4 fabrics, cut:

4 strips, 2" x 42"; crosscut into:
    4 rectangles, 2" x 10½" (8 total)
    8 rectangles, 2" x 9" (16 total)
    4 rectangles, 2" x 7½" (8 total)
1 strip, 3" x 42"; crosscut into:
    3 rectangles, 3" x 6½" (6 total)
    3 rectangles, 3" x 5" (6 total)
1 strip, 1½" x 42"; crosscut into:
    3 rectangles, 1½" x 7½" (6 total)
    3 rectangles, 1½" x 4" (6 total)
3 squares, 4" x 4" (6 total)

From *each* of the binding fabrics, cut:

4 strips, 8½" x 42" (8 total)

Large Quilt Option

To make 60 blocks (30 in each color combination and 12 of each setting triangle) for a quilt measuring 80" x 80", you'll need:

5 yards *total* of A fabrics (lightest) for blocks
5 yards *total* of D fabrics (darkest) for blocks
1⅓ yards *each* of 2 fabrics (1 light and
    1 dark) for binding
5 yards of fabric for backing
86" x 86" piece of batting

PIECING THE BLOCKS

Once the blocks are pieced, they'll be sliced in half diagonally. For each group of rectangles around the center square, I opted to use one fabric so that when the blocks are sliced, the fabrics create a unified triangle. After each addition, press the seam allowances toward the D fabric. This will help the seams nest when you sew the center diagonal seam.

1. Starting with a D square, sew a 1½" x 4" A rectangle to the bottom of the square. Sew a matching 3" x 5" A rectangle to the left side of the unit. Add a matching 3" x 6½" A rectangle to the top of the unit and then add a matching 1½" x 7½" A rectangle to the right side of the unit. Make 12 units.

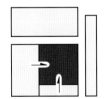

Make 12.

2. Sew a 2" x 7½" D rectangle to the bottom of the unit from step 1. Sew matching 2" x 9" D rectangles to the left side and then the top of the unit. Add a matching 2" x 10½" D

rectangle to the right side of the unit to complete the block. Make 12 blocks.

Make 12.

3. Repeat step 1, starting with an A square and adding D rectangles.
4. Repeat step 2, sewing A rectangles to the unit from step 3 to complete the block. Make 12 blocks.
5. At your cutting mat, carefully cut each block in half diagonally to make 24 half-blocks with dark outer edges and 24 half-blocks with light outer edges.

 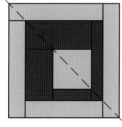

Cut.   Cut.

6. Carefully pin each dark half-block to a light half-block, matching the seams as you pin. Sew the half-blocks together, being careful not to stretch the bias edges. Press the seam allowances to one side. Trim the blocks to measure 10" x 10". Make 12 blocks of each color combination.

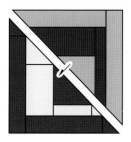 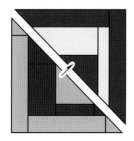

Make 12 of each.

ASSEMBLING THE QUILT TOP

1. Lay out the blocks and quarter-square triangles, rotating them as shown in the quilt assembly diagram below. Pin and sew the blocks together in diagonal rows. Press the seam allowances in opposite directions from row to row.
2. Pin and sew the rows together to complete the quilt top. Press the seam allowances in one direction.

Quilt assembly

PREPARING THE QUILT LAYERS

1. Cut the length of the backing fabric into one 60"-long piece and one 30"-long piece. Cut the 30"-long piece in half lengthwise. Sew the two 30"-long pieces end to end to make a 60"-long piece. Join the two 60"-long

25

pieces side by side and press the seam allowances open.

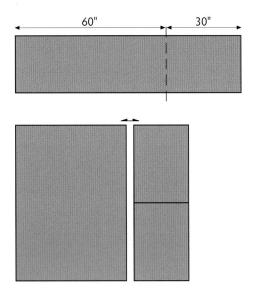

2. Referring to "Basting a Quilt Sandwich" on page 77, layer the backing, batting, and quilt top; then baste the layers together. Use your favorite quilting technique to quilt a design that you love.

ADDING A WIDE BINDING

I opted to frame the quilt with a wide binding (cutting my strips 8½" wide) and change the colors of the binding at the mitered corners. To use my technique, be sure to ask your quilter *not* to trim the batting and backing if you want to add a wide binding; you'll trim it after attaching the binding.

1. Sew the four light strips together end to end with a diagonal seam and press the seam allowances open. Join the four dark strips in the same way. Fold each long strip in half lengthwise, with wrong sides together, and press.

2. Starting at a corner and leaving a 4" to 6" tail for mitering, begin sewing ¼" from the quilt edge, using a ¼"-wide seam allowance.

3. When you arrive at the next corner, stop sewing ¼" from the quilt edge with a backstitch. Remove the quilt from the machine

and trim the binding leaving a 4" to 6" tail. Fold the binding tail away from the quilt top. Continue as before, switching colors of binding as indicated in the photo on page 22.

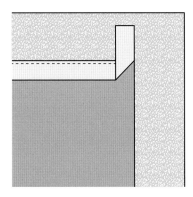

4. Using a rotary cutter and long ruler, trim the batting and backing 2" from the stitched line. Do not trim the binding tails.

5. To form the miters, measure the binding from the fold to the seam line; it should be about 4". Divide the measurement in half, and mark the midpoint on the binding. On the binding tail, draw a 45° line from the stitching line to the midpoint. Then draw a 45° line from the midpoint to the folded edge as shown; this will be the stitching line.

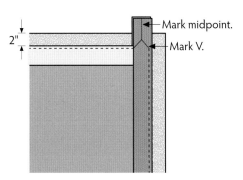

6. Carefully fold back the quilt, on the diagonal, and pin the binding tails together. Using a small stitch length and starting with a backstitch, sew along the marked line, pivoting at the midpoint, and stopping with a backstitch. Trim the excess fabric, leaving a ¼" seam allowance. Clip the corner of the binding as needed, and fold the binding over the corner to the back of the quilt. Finish by hand as usual.

26

quadrille

FINISHED QUILT: 63½" x 72½"
FINISHED BLOCK: 9" x 9"

MATERIALS

Yardage is based on 42"-wide fabric.

3⅞ yards *total* of 3 assorted A fabrics (lightest)
   for blocks
1⅛ yards of D fabric (darkest) for blocks
⅞ yard of B fabric (medium) for blocks
⅔ yard of C fabric (medium) for blocks
⅝ yard of fabric for binding
4 yards of fabric for backing
69" x 78" piece of batting

CUTTING

From the assorted A fabrics, cut *a total of:*
2 strips, 8" x 42"; crosscut into 7 squares, 8" x 8"
11 strips, 6½" x 42"; crosscut into 112 rectangles,
   3½" x 6½"
1 strip, 5" x 42"; crosscut into 7 squares, 5" x 5"
3 strips, 3½" x 42"; crosscut into 56 rectangles,
   2" x 3½"
3 strips, 2" x 42"; crosscut into 56 squares, 2" x 2"

From the B fabric, cut:
3 strips, 5" x 42"; crosscut into: 56 rectangles,
   2" x 5"
3 strips, 3½" x 42"; crosscut into 56 rectangles,
   2" x 3½"

From the C fabric, cut:
2 strips, 8" x 42"; crosscut into 7 squares, 8" x 8"
1 strip, 5" x 42"; crosscut into 7 squares, 5" x 5"

From the D fabric, cut:
3 strips, 6½" x 42"; crosscut into 56 rectangles,
   2" x 6½"
3 strips, 5" x 42"; crosscut into 56 rectangles,
   2" x 5"

From the binding fabric, cut:
7 strips, 2½" x 42"

"*Quadrille" is made with quarter Log Cabin blocks that I updated with the addition of half-square-triangle units. The blocks can be turned in any number of ways to achieve your own unique look—the results are just as fun as the process!*

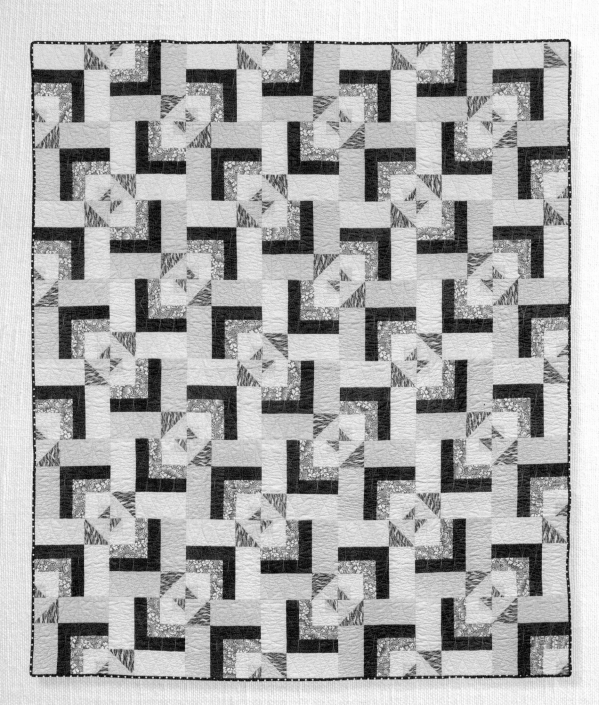

Designed and pieced by Amy Ellis; machine quilted by Natalia Bonner

PIECING THE BLOCKS

1. To make half-square-triangle units, draw intersecting diagonal lines on the wrong side of each 5" A square. Layer each marked square with a 5" C square, right sides together. Sew ¼" on each side of both drawn lines.

2. Cut the squares apart horizontally and vertically. Then cut the squares on the drawn diagonal lines to make 56 half-square-triangle units. Press the seam allowances toward the C triangle. Trim the units to measure 2" square.

Make 56.

3. Repeat steps 1 and 2, using the 8" A and C squares to make 56 half-square-triangle units. Trim the units to measure 3½" square.

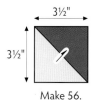

Make 56.

4. Pin and sew a 2" A square to a 2" half-square-triangle unit as shown in the diagram following step 7. Press the seam allowances toward the A square. Sew a 2" x 3½" A rectangle to the top of the unit and press the seam allowances toward the A rectangle.

5. Pin and sew a 2" x 3½" B rectangle to the right side of the unit from step 4. Then sew a 2" x 5" B rectangle to the top of the unit. Press the seam allowances toward the newly added rectangles.

6. Pin and sew a 2" x 5" D rectangle to the right side of the unit from step 5. Then sew a 2" x 6½" D rectangle to the top of the unit. Press the seam allowances toward the newly added rectangles.

7. Pin and sew a 3½" x 6½" A rectangle to the top of the unit from step 6. Press the seam allowances toward the D rectangle. Make 56 units.

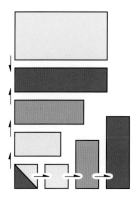 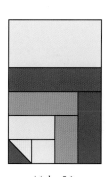

Make 56.

8. Pin and sew a 3½" half-square-triangle unit to one end of a 3½" x 6½" A rectangle. Press the seam allowances toward the half-square-triangle unit. Make 56.

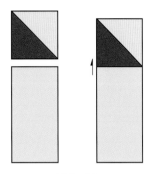

Make 56.

9. Pin and sew the unit from step 7 to the unit from step 8 to complete the block. Press the seam allowances to one side. Make 56.

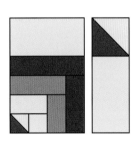 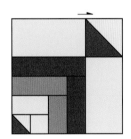

Make 56.

ASSEMBLING THE QUILT TOP

1. Lay out eight rows of seven blocks each, rotating the blocks as shown in the quilt assembly diagram at right, or in any arrangement you desire. Pin and sew the blocks together in rows, pressing the seam allowances in opposite directions from row to row.

2. Pin and sew the rows together to complete the quilt top. Press the seam allowances in one direction.

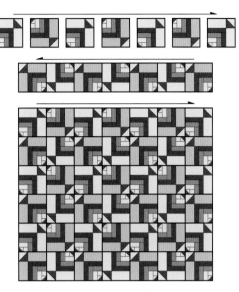

Quilt assembly

FINISHING THE QUILT

1. Cut the length of the backing fabric in half to create two 72"-long pieces. Sew the two pieces together side by side and press the seam allowances open.

2. Referring to "Basting a Quilt Sandwich" on page 77, layer the backing, batting, and quilt top; then baste the layers together. Use your favorite quilting technique to quilt a design that you love.

3. Referring to "Binding" on page 78 and using the 2½"-wide strips, bind your quilt.

placid curves

FINISHED QUILT: 84½" x 96½"
FINISHED BLOCK: 12" x 12"

The subtle color variations in "Placid Curves," made of squares and rectangles, trick the eye into seeing curves. I love the movement in this quilt and the simplicity. Take care when cutting segments and making the strip sets; your choices will make all the difference when it's time to assemble the blocks.

MATERIALS

Yardage is based on 42"-wide fabric.

5¼ yards *total* of assorted B fabrics (medium) for blocks
5 yards *total* of assorted A fabrics (lightest) for blocks
⅞ yard of fabric for binding
8 yards of fabric for backing
90" x 102" piece of batting

CUTTING

From the assorted A fabrics, cut *a total of:*
9 strips, 5" x 42"
13 strips, 3" x 42"
9 strips, 2½" x 42"
13 strips, 2" x 42"
9 strips, 1½" x 42"
13 strips, 1" x 42"

From the assorted B fabrics, cut *a total of:*
13 strips, 5" x 42"
9 strips, 3" x 42"
13 strips, 2½" x 42"
9 strips, 2" x 42"
13 strips, 1½" x 42"
9 strips, 1" x 42"

From the binding fabric, cut:
10 strips, 2½" x 42"

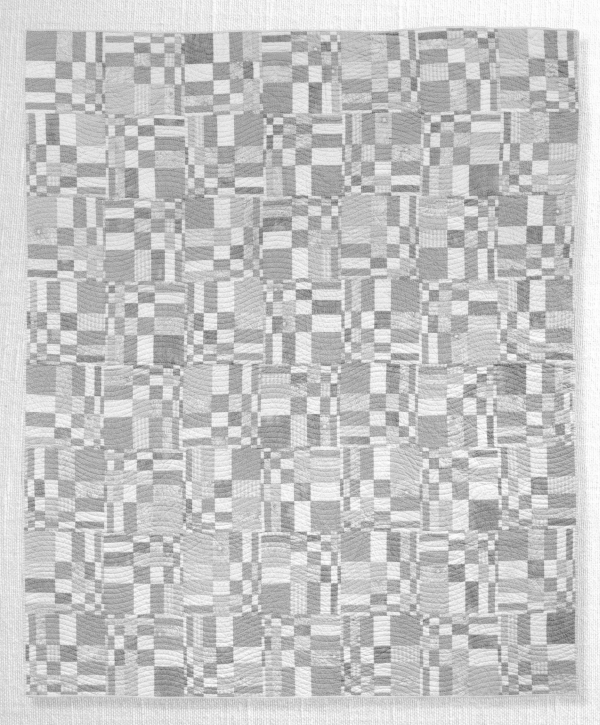

Designed by Amy Ellis; pieced by Audrie Bidwell; machine quilted by Natalia Bonner

Squaring the Edge of Your Fabric

Squaring up your fabric is a necessary step prior to cutting strips; otherwise the strips will be cut on a slant. Crooked strips can be a problem when cutting smaller pieces for your quilt as you may not be able to cut enough pieces from the allotted fabric. Square up each new length of fabric on a cutting mat. Verify that the fabric edge is square before cutting the next strip.

1. Fold the fabric selvage to selvage.
2. Before laying the fabric down on the cutting mat, slide the selvages left or right until the fold of the fabric is flat. The cut edges of the fabric will most likely not be together.
3. Place the folded edge closest to you along a line on the cutting mat.
4. Align a small ruler along the folded edge of the fabric. Place a long ruler at the left edge of the smaller ruler, just covering the uneven raw edges of the fabric. Remove the smaller ruler and cut along the right-hand edge of the long ruler. Discard this strip.

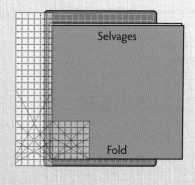

PIECING THE BLOCKS

This block is made from two strip sets. While cutting, you probably noticed a few similarities in the width of the strips. Use care when sewing and cutting the segments for the best results. Press all seam allowances toward the B fabric.

1. Sew the 1"-wide B strips to the 1½"-wide A strips.
2. Sew the 2"-wide B strips to the 2½"-wide A strips.
3. Sew the 3"-wide B strips to the 5"-wide A strips.
4. Sew the strips from steps 1–3 together to complete nine A strip sets as shown.

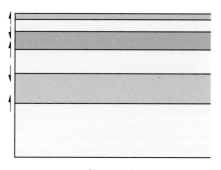

Strip set A.
Make 9.

5. Sew the 1"-wide A strips to the 1½"-wide B strips.

6. Sew the 2"-wide A strips to the 2½"-wide B strips.

7. Sew the 3"-wide A strips to the 5"-wide B strips.

8. Sew the strips from steps 5–7 together to complete 13 B strip sets as shown.

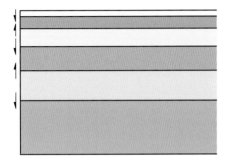

Strip set B.
Make 13.

9. From the A strip sets, cut 3"-wide, 2"-wide, and 1"-wide segments. Cut 56 segments of *each* width.

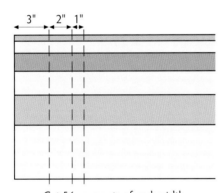

Cut 56 segments of each width.

10. From the B strip sets, cut 5"-wide, 2½"-wide, and 1½"-wide segments. Cut 56 segments of *each* width.

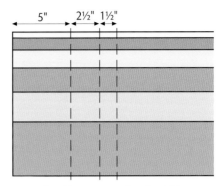

Cut 56 segments of each width.

11. Arrange the A and B segments as shown. Pin and sew the segments together to complete a block. Press the seam allowances in one direction. Make 56 blocks.

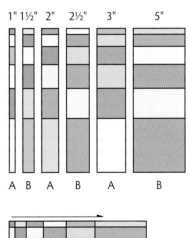

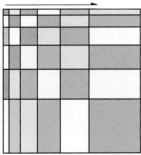

Make 56.

ASSEMBLING THE QUILT TOP

1. Lay out eight rows of seven blocks each, rotating the blocks as shown in the quilt assembly diagram below. Pin and sew the blocks together in rows, pressing the seam allowances in opposite directions from row to row.

2. Pin and sew the rows together to complete the quilt top. Press the seam allowances in one direction.

FINISHING THE QUILT

1. Cut the length of the backing fabric into three 95"-long pieces. Sew the three pieces together side by side and press the seam allowances open.

2. Referring to "Basting a Quilt Sandwich" on page 77, layer the backing, batting, and quilt top; then baste the layers together. Use your favorite quilting technique to quilt a design that you love.

3. Referring to "Binding" on page 78 and using the 2½"-wide strips, bind your quilt.

Quilt assembly

Designed and pieced by Amy Ellis; machine quilted by Natalia Bonner

whispered lace

FINISHED QUILT: 96½" x 96½"
FINISHED BLOCK: 16" x 16"

"Whispered Lace" is one of my favorite quilts in this book. Gather a variety of fabrics and unite the blocks with white or cream "sashing" used consistently throughout the quilt. While this is a large quilt, the oversized blocks make it a quick piecing project. Enjoy!

MATERIALS

Yardage is based on 42"-wide fabric.

5½ yards of A fabric (lightest) for blocks
⅔ yard *each* of 12 assorted B fabrics (medium) for blocks
⅞ yard of fabric for binding
9 yards of fabric for backing
102" x 102" piece of batting

CUTTING

Choose 6 B fabrics for block 1 and 6 B fabrics for block 2.

From the A fabric, cut:
6 strips, 12½" x 42"; crosscut into 144 rectangles, 1½" x 12½"
3 strips, 7" x 42"; crosscut into 72 rectangles, 1½" x 7"
3 strips, 4½" x 42"; crosscut into 72 rectangles, 1½" x 4½"
3 strips, 4" x 42"; crosscut into 72 rectangles, 1½" x 4"
6 strips, 3½" x 42"; crosscut into 144 rectangles, 1½" x 3½"
5 strips, 2½" x 42"; crosscut into 108 rectangles, 1½" x 2½"
18 strips, 1½" x 42"

Continued on page 38

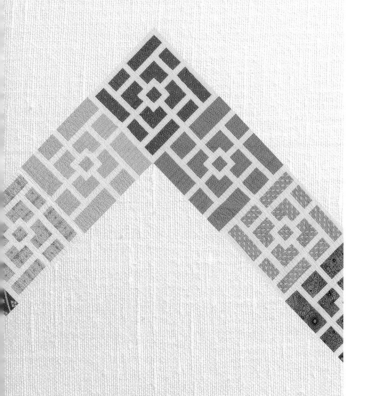

From *each* of the 6 B fabrics for block 1, cut:

1 strip, 2½" x 42"; crosscut into:
    6 rectangles, 2½" x 4" (36 total)
    3 squares, 2½" x 2½" (18 total)
1 strip, 8" x 42" (6 total)
2 strips, 4" x 42" (12 total)
1 strip, 2" x 42" (6 total)

From *each* of the 6 B fabrics for block 2, cut:

1 strip, 7" x 42"; crosscut into 12 rectangles,
    2½" x 7" (72 total)
2 strips, 4" x 42"; crosscut *1 of the strips* into
    12 rectangles, 2½" x 4" (72 total)
1 strip, 2½" x 42"; crosscut into:
    6 rectangles, 2½" x 4" (36 total)
    3 squares, 2½" x 2½" (18 total)
1 strip, 2" x 42" (6 total)

From the binding fabric, cut:

10 strips, 2½" x 42"

PIECING THE BLOCKS

Press all seam allowances toward the A pieces, unless directed otherwise. (I like the A pieces to pop up a little with the extra bulk from the seam allowances.) The block centers are all pieced the same way; however, there are separate directions for completing block A and block B.

1. Sew 1½" x 2½" A rectangles to opposite sides of each 2½" B square. Sew 1½" x 4½" A rectangles to the remaining two sides of the square to complete the center unit.

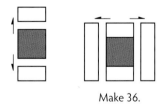

Make 36.

2. Sew a 1½"-wide A strip between matching 2"-wide and 4"-wide B strips as shown. Press the seam allowances toward the A strip. Make one strip set of each B fabric (12 total). From *each* strip set, cut 9 segments, 2½" wide.

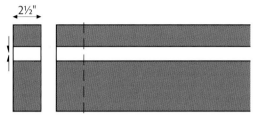

Make 1 strip set with each B fabric (12 total).
Cut 9 segments from each.

3. From each group of matching B segments, trim three segments to measure 4½" long, making sure the A strip is centered as shown.

Trim 3 of each group of matching segments.

4. Sew a trimmed unit from step 3 to the bottom of a matching center unit. Sew matching segments from step 2 to the left side, and then to the top of the center unit as shown.

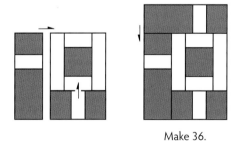

Make 36.

5. Sew matching 2½" x 4" B rectangles to both sides of a 1½" x 2½" A rectangle. Make three matching units from each B fabric (36 total).

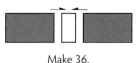

Make 36.

6. Sew a unit from step 5 to a matching unit from step 4 as shown to complete the center unit. Make 36 units.

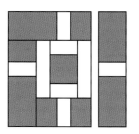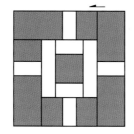

Make 36.

Block 1

Use the B fabrics cut for block 1.

1. Sew a 1½"-wide A strip between matching 4"-wide and 8"-wide B strips as shown. Press the seam allowances toward the A strip. Make six strip sets. From each strip set, cut 12 segments, 3½" wide.

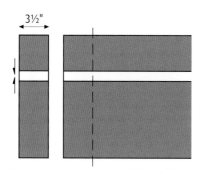

Make 1 strip set with each B fabric (6 total).
Cut 12 segments from each.

2. Pin and sew a 1½" x 12½" A rectangle to the left side of each segment from step 1 as shown. Press the seam allowances toward the A rectangle. Make 12 of each B fabric.

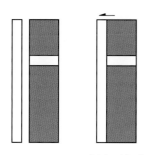

Make 12 of
each B fabric.

3. Lay out four units from step 2 and a center unit, all matching. Sew a step 2 unit to the bottom of a center unit, stitching about 6" across the edge as shown.

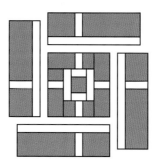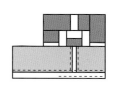

4. Working in a counterclockwise direction, sew a unit to the right edge of the center unit. Press the seam allowances toward the A rectangle. Then sew a third unit to the top edge; press. Sew a unit to the left edge of the unit; press. Complete the partial seam stitched in step 3 to complete the block. Make 18 blocks.

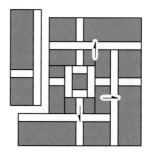

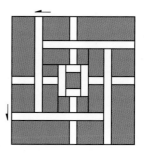

Block 1.
Make 18.

Block 2

Use the B fabrics cut for block 2.

1. Sew a 1½" x 4" A rectangle to the right edge of a 2½" x 4" B rectangle. Press the seam allowances toward the A rectangle. Sew a 1½" x 3½" A rectangle to the bottom of the unit. Press the seam allowances toward the B rectangle. Make 12 of each B fabric.

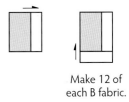

Make 12 of
each B fabric.

2. Sew a 1½" x 7" A rectangle to the right edge of a 2½" x 7" B rectangle. Press the seam allowances toward the A rectangle. Sew a 1½" x 3½" A rectangle to the bottom of the unit. Press the seam allowances toward the A rectangle. Make 12 of each B fabric.

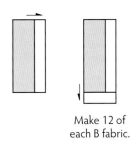

Make 12 of
each B fabric.

3. Sew the units from steps 1 and 2 together as shown. Press the seam allowances toward the B rectangle. Sew a 1½" x 12½" A rectangle to the left side of the unit and press the seam allowances toward the A rectangle. Make 12 of each B fabric.

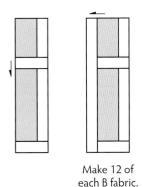

Make 12 of
each B fabric.

4. Referring to steps 3 and 4 for block 1 and working in a counterclockwise direction, sew four matching units from step 3 to a matching center unit to make a block. Press the seam allowances toward the A rectangles. Make 18 blocks.

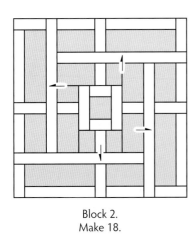

Block 2.
Make 18.

ASSEMBLING THE QUILT TOP

1. Lay out six rows of six blocks each, alternating the 1 and 2 blocks as shown in the quilt assembly diagram, opposite. Pin and sew the blocks together in rows, pressing the seam allowances in opposite directions from row to row.
2. Sew the rows together to complete the quilt top. Press the seam allowances in one direction.

FINISHING THE QUILT

1. Cut the length of the backing fabric into three 108"-long pieces. Sew the three pieces together side by side and press the seam allowances open.
2. Referring to "Basting a Quilt Sandwich" on page 77, layer the backing, batting, and quilt top; then baste the layers together. Use your favorite quilting technique to quilt a design that you love.
3. Referring to "Binding" on page 78 and using the 2½"-wide strips, bind your quilt.

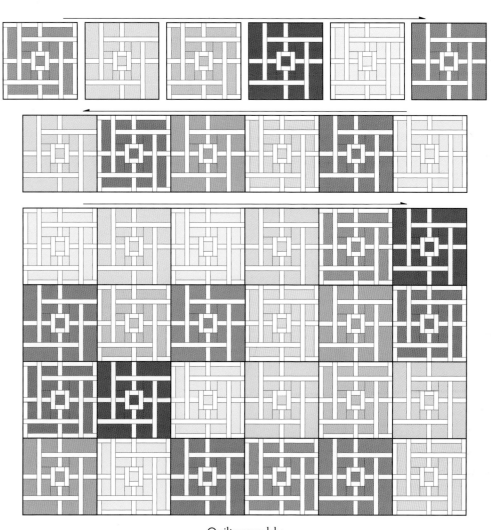

Quilt assembly

Designed and pieced by Amy Ellis; machine quilted by Natalia Bonner

in motion

FINISHED QUILT: 72½" x 72½"
FINISHED BLOCK: 12" x 12"

MATERIALS

Yardage is based on 42"-wide fabric.

3½ yards *total* of assorted A fabrics (lightest)
   for blocks
1 yard of B1 fabric (medium) for blocks
1 yard of B2 fabric (medium) for blocks
1 yard of C1 fabric (medium) for blocks
1 yard of C2 fabric (medium) for blocks
1 yard of D1 fabric (darkest) for blocks
1 yard of D2 fabric (darkest) for blocks
⅔ yard of fabric for binding
4½ yards of fabric for backing
78" x 78" piece of batting

Baby Quilt Option

To make 16 blocks for a quilt measuring
48½" x 48½", you'll need:

1⅝ yards of A fabric (lightest) for blocks
⅝ yard of B fabric (medium) for blocks
⅝ yard *each* of 2 D fabrics (darkest)
   for blocks
⅜ yard of B1 fabric (medium) for blocks
⅜ yard *each* of 2 C fabrics (medium)
   for blocks
½ yard of fabric for binding
3 yards of fabric for backing
54" x 54" piece of batting

"In Motion" is a long-term project, best made without a time frame in mind so that you're able to enjoy the process as you work through all the pieces. In the end, the results are absolutely worth the effort. Choose one fabric for each grouping and make notes as you cut; keeping the pieces organized will be helpful as you work.

CUTTING

From the assorted A fabrics, cut *a total of:*

16 strips, 6" x 42"; crosscut into 96 squares,
  6" x 6"*

7 strips, 2½" x 42"; crosscut into 108 squares,
  2½" x 2½"

From the B1 fabric, cut:

3 strips, 6" x 42"; crosscut into 18 squares,
  6" x 6"*

5 strips, 2½" x 42"; crosscut into 72 squares,
  2½" x 2½"

From the B2 fabric, cut:

3 strips, 6" x 42"; crosscut into 14 squares,
  6" x 6"*

5 strips, 2½" x 42"; crosscut into 72 squares,
  2½" x 2½"

From *each* of the C1 and C2 fabrics, cut:

3 strips, 6" x 42"; crosscut into 14 squares,
  6" x 6"* (28 total)

5 strips, 2½" x 42"; crosscut into 72 squares,
  2½" x 2½" (144 total)

From *each* of the D1 and D2 fabrics, cut:

3 strips, 6" x 42"; crosscut into 18 squares,
  6" x 6"* (36 total)

5 strips, 2½" x 42"; crosscut into 72 squares,
  2½" x 2½" (144 total)

From the binding fabric, cut:

8 strips, 2½" x 42"

*If you're using a GO! cutter, don't cut these
pieces. See "Ready, Set, GO!" at right instead.*

PIECING THE BLOCKS

This block is full of half-square-triangle units. The
number of units required may seem a bit over-
whelming, but just take your time and enjoy the
process. Your units will be multiplying in no time.

1. To make half-square-triangle units, draw
   intersecting diagonal lines on the wrong side
   of each 6" A square. Layer a marked square

with each 6" B square, right sides together.
Sew ¼" on each side of both drawn lines.

2. Cut the squares apart horizontally and
   vertically. Then cut the squares on the drawn
   diagonal lines to make 144 half-square-
   triangle units. Press the seam allowances
   and trim the units to measure 2½" square.

   The seam allowances of the half-square-
   triangle units on the left side of the block are
   pressed toward the dark fabric, while the
   seam allowances in units on the right need
   to be pressed toward the light fabric. This
   will help the seams nest when assembling
   the block.

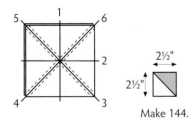

Make 144.

3. Repeat steps 1 and 2, using the marked A squares and the 6" B2, C1, C2, D1, and D2 squares to make half-square-triangle units in the quantity indicated. Press the seam allowances and trim the units to measure 2½" square. (You'll have four extra each of B2, C1, and C2 units.)

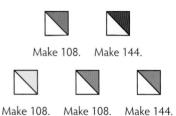

Make 108.   Make 144.

Make 108.   Make 108.   Make 144.

4. Lay out the 2½" B1, B2, C1, C2, D1 and D2 squares and the half-square-triangle units in six rows as shown. Sew the pieces together into rows, pressing the seam allowances in opposite directions from row to row.

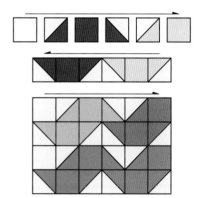

5. Sew the rows together to complete the block. Press the seam allowances in one direction. Make 36 blocks.

Make 36.

ASSEMBLING THE QUILT TOP

1. Lay out six rows of six blocks each, rotating the blocks as shown below. Pin and sew the blocks together in rows, pressing the seam allowances in opposite directions from row to row.

2. Sew the rows together to complete the quilt top. Press the seam allowances in one direction.

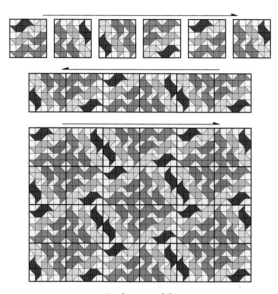

Quilt assembly

FINISHING THE QUILT

1. Cut the length of the backing fabric in half to create two 80"-long pieces. Sew the two pieces together side by side and press the seam allowances open.

2. Referring to "Basting a Quilt Sandwich" on page 77, layer the backing, batting, and quilt top; then baste the layers together. Use your favorite quilting technique to quilt a design that you love.

3. Referring to "Binding" on page 78 and using the 2½"-wide strips, bind your quilt.

Designed by Amy Ellis; pieced by Trish Poolson; machine quilted by Natalia Bonner

prism

FINISHED QUILT: 63½" x 81½"
FINISHED BLOCK: 9" x 9"

I love the stark contrast and dominant shapes that emerge when these crisp blocks are turned and sewn into a quilt top. "Prism" is stunning and actually quite easy to make! Take time to accurately cut the triangles so that they match up easily when assembling the blocks.

MATERIALS

Yardage is based on 42"-wide fabric.

3¼ yards of A fabric (lightest) for blocks
3¼ yards of D fabric (darkest) for blocks
1⅝ yards of B fabric (medium) for blocks
⅔ yard of fabric for binding
5 yards of fabric for backing
69" x 87" piece of batting

CUTTING

From the A fabric, cut:
4 strips, 7¼" x 42"; crosscut into 16 squares, 7¼" x 7¼". Cut the squares into quarters diagonally to yield 64 triangles (1 is extra).
7 strips, 10½" x 42"; crosscut into 126 rectangles, 2" x 10½"

From the D fabric, cut:
4 strips, 7¼" x 42"; crosscut into 16 squares, 7¼" x 7¼". Cut the squares into quarters diagonally to yield 64 triangles (1 is extra).
7 strips, 10½" x 42"; crosscut into 126 rectangles, 2" x 10½"

From the B fabric, cut:
7 strips, 7¼" x 42"; crosscut into 32 squares, 7¼" x 7¼". Cut the squares into quarters diagonally to yield 128 triangles (2 are extra).

From the binding fabric, cut:
8 strips, 2½" x 42"

PIECING THE BLOCKS

1. Fold an A rectangle in half and finger-press to mark the center of the long side. Fold a D triangle in half and finger-press to mark the center of the long side. Sew the triangle to the rectangle, matching the center creases. Press the seam allowances toward the D triangle. Make 63 units.

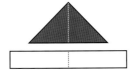

Make 63.

2. Using the same techniques as step 1, center and sew A triangles to 63 D rectangles as shown. Center and sew 63 B triangles to the remaining D rectangles. Center and sew the remaining B triangles to the remaining A rectangles. Press the seam allowances in the direction indicated by the arrows. Make 63 of each color combination.

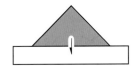

Make 63 of each.

3. Using a ruler, trim the ends of the rectangles even with the sides of the triangle as shown.

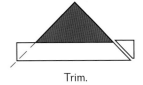

Trim.

4. Pin and sew two units from step 3 together as shown, making sure to match the seam intersections. Press the seam allowances as indicated. Make 63 of each.

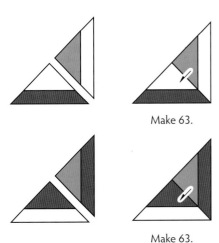

Make 63.

Make 63.

5. Pin and sew the units from step 4 together in pairs to complete the blocks. Press the seam allowances in one direction. Make 63 blocks.

Make 63.

Bias Edges

Cutting all those squares into triangles is easy enough, but sewing the bias edges together can offer a few challenges if you aren't careful. When I'm working with bias edges, I use a little spray starch before cutting to keep the fabrics stiff. When sewing the quarter triangles together, use pins and sew from the center point out. The band of non-bias strips around the block will help keep the bias in check.

ASSEMBLING THE QUILT TOP

1. Lay out nine rows of seven blocks each, rotating the blocks as shown in the quilt assembly diagram below. Pin and sew the blocks together in rows, pressing the seam allowances in opposite directions from row to row.

2. Sew the rows together to complete the quilt top. Press the seam allowances in one direction.

FINISHING THE QUILT

1. Cut the length of the backing fabric in half to create two 90"-long pieces. Sew the two pieces together side by side and press the seam allowances open.

2. Referring to "Basting a Quilt Sandwich" on page 77, layer the backing, batting, and quilt top; then baste the layers together. Use your favorite quilting technique to quilt a design that you love.

3. Referring to "Binding" on page 78 and using the 2½"-wide strips, bind your quilt.

Quilt assembly

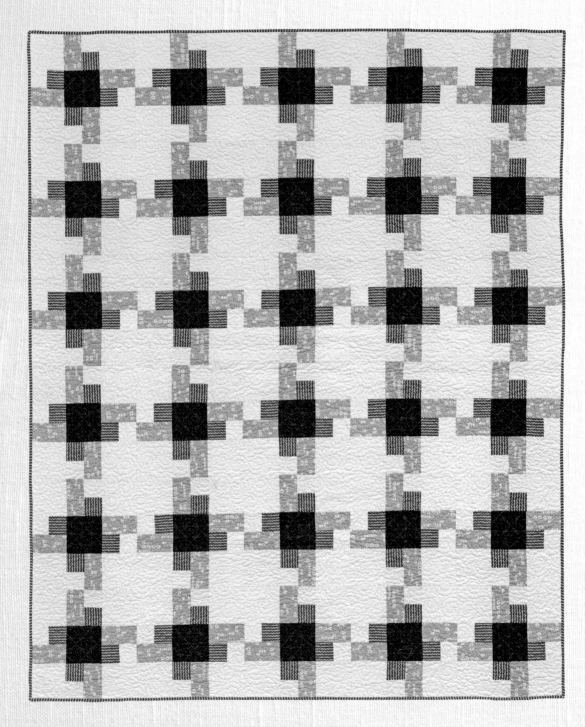

Designed by Amy Ellis; pieced by Sherri McConnell; machine quilted by Natalia Bonner

digital pinwheel

FINISHED QUILT: 60½" x 72½"
FINISHED BLOCK: 12" x 12"

The simplicity of "Digital Pinwheel" makes for a striking quilt. I love how the subtle variation of tone creates movement and keeps your eye moving over the quilt. Carefully choose your fabrics for the right amount of contrast and enjoy the process.

MATERIALS

Yardage is based on 42"-wide fabric.

2⅞ yards of A fabric (lightest) for blocks
1⅛ yards of B fabric (medium) for blocks
⅝ yard of D fabric (darkest) for blocks
⅔ yard of C fabric (medium) for blocks
⅝ yard of fabric for binding
4 yards of fabric for backing
66" x 78" piece of batting

CUTTING

From the A fabric, cut:
15 strips, 4½" x 42"; crosscut into 120 squares, 4½" x 4½"
8 strips, 2½" x 42"

From the C fabric, cut:
8 strips, 2½" x 42"

From the B fabric, cut:
8 strips, 4½" x 42"; crosscut into 120 rectangles, 2½" x 4½"

From the D fabric, cut:
4 strips, 4½" x 42"; crosscut into 30 squares, 4½" x 4½"

From the binding fabric, cut:
7 strips, 2½" x 42"

51

Baby Quilt Option

To make 12 blocks for a quilt measuring 36½" x 48½", you'll need:

1⅛ yards of A fabric (lightest) for blocks
½ yard of B fabric (medium) for blocks
⅓ yard of C fabric (medium) for blocks
⅓ yard of D fabric (darkest) for blocks
½ yard of fabric for binding
1½ yards of fabric for backing
42" x 54" piece of batting

PIECING THE BLOCKS

1. Sew an A strip to a C strip. Press the seam allowances toward the C strip. Make eight strip sets. Cut the strip sets into 120 segments, 2½" wide.

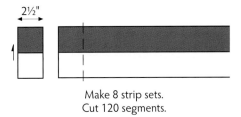

Make 8 strip sets.
Cut 120 segments.

2. Pin and sew a B rectangle to the right side of each segment from step 1. Press the seam allowances toward the B rectangle. Make 120 units.

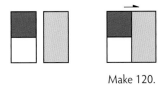

Make 120.

3. Pin and sew A squares to opposite sides of a unit from step 2 as shown. Press the seam allowances toward the A squares. Make 60 of row A.

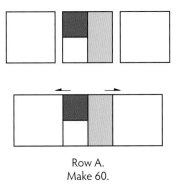

Row A.
Make 60.

4. Pin and sew a D square between two units from step 2 as shown. Press the seam allowances toward the D square. Make 30 of row B.

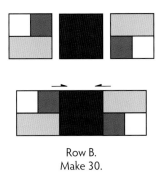

Row B.
Make 30.

5. Pin and sew two of row A and one of row B together to make a block. Press the seam allowances toward row B. Make 30 blocks.

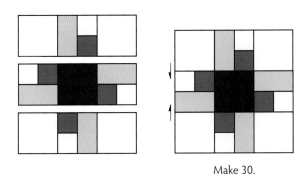

Make 30.

ASSEMBLING THE QUILT TOP

1. Lay out six rows of five blocks each as shown in the quilt assembly diagram below. Pin and sew the blocks together in rows, pressing the seam allowances in opposite directions from row to row.

2. Pin and sew the rows together to complete the quilt top. Press the seam allowances in one direction.

FINISHING THE QUILT

1. Cut the length of the backing fabric in half to create two 72"-long pieces. Sew the two pieces together side by side and press the seam allowances open.

2. Referring to "Basting a Quilt Sandwich" on page 77, layer the backing, batting, and quilt top; then baste the layers together. Use your favorite quilting technique to quilt a design that you love.

3. Referring to "Binding" on page 78 and using the 2½"-wide strips, bind your quilt.

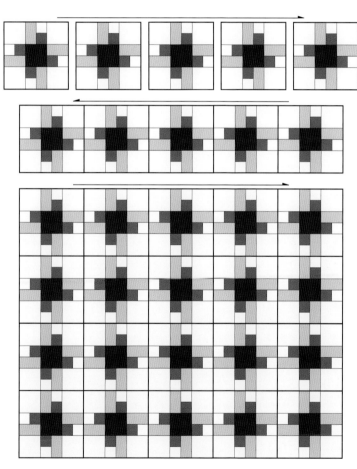

Quilt assembly

Designed and pieced by Amy Ellis; machine quilted by Natalia Bonner

double diamonds

FINISHED QUILT: 60½" x 72½"
FINISHED BLOCK: 12" x 12"

It's true—inspiration can strike at any time! "Double Diamonds" was inspired by a woven blanket I saw one evening while watching television. I quickly snapped a picture of the screen so I could later figure out how to incorporate the shapes of the blanket into a quilt. I love the results! Be sure to carefully sew and trim, as needed, for great-fitting blocks.

MATERIALS

Yardage is based on 42"-wide fabric.

4 yards of A fabric (lightest) for blocks
2½ yards of D fabric (darkest) for blocks
⅝ yard of fabric for binding
4 yards of fabric for backing
66" x 78" piece of batting

CUTTING

From the A fabric, cut:

4 strips, 8½" x 42"; crosscut into 60 rectangles, 2½" x 8½"
3 strips, 6" x 42"; crosscut into 15 squares, 6" x 6"
5 strips, 5¼" x 42"; crosscut into 30 squares, 5¼" x 5¼". Cut the squares into quarters diagonally to yield 120 triangles.
4 strips, 4½" x 42"; crosscut into 60 rectangles, 2½" x 4½"
10 strips, 2⅞" x 42"; crosscut into 120 squares, 2⅞" x 2⅞". Cut the squares in half diagonally to yield 240 triangles.
2 strips, 2½" x 42"; crosscut into 30 squares, 2½" x 2½"

From the D fabric, cut:

3 strips, 6" x 42"; crosscut into 15 squares, 6" x 6"
3 strips, 5¼" x 42"; crosscut into 15 squares, 5¼" x 5¼". Cut the squares into quarters diagonally to yield 60 triangles.
4 strips, 4½" x 42"; crosscut into 60 rectangles, 2½" x 4½"
6 strips, 3⅜" x 42"; crosscut into 60 squares, 3⅜" x 3⅜"
3 strips, 3¼" x 42"; crosscut into 30 squares, 3¼" x 3¼". Cut the squares into quarters diagonally to yield 120 triangles.

From the binding fabric, cut:

7 strips, 2½" x 42"

PIECING THE BLOCKS

1. Fold a 2⅞" A triangle in half and finger-press to mark the center of the long side. Repeat for a total of four triangles. Fold a 3⅜" D square into quarters and finger-press to mark the centers of the sides. Sew the triangles to opposite sides of the square, matching the center creases. Press the seam allowances in the same direction. Center and sew triangles to the remaining sides of the square; press. Make 60 units.

 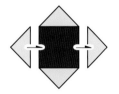

Make 60.

2. Using the same technique as step 1, center and sew two 3¼" D triangles to opposite sides of a 2½" A square. Press the seam allowances in the same direction. Center and sew D triangles to the remaining sides of the square; press. Make 30 units.

Make 30.

3. To make half-square-triangle units, draw intersecting diagonal lines on the wrong side of each 6" A square. Layer each marked square with a 6" D square, right sides together. Sew ¼" on each side of both drawn lines.

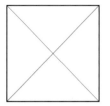 

4. Cut the squares apart horizontally and vertically. Then cut the squares on the drawn diagonal lines to make 120 half-square-triangle units. Press the seam allowances and trim the units to measure 2½" square.

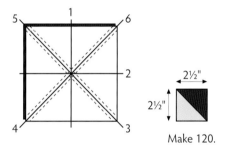

Make 120.

5. Sew two units from step 1 together as shown, rotating one unit as needed so the seams nest. Press the seam allowances in one direction. Make 30 units.

Make 30.

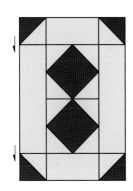

Reading Seams

Not that there are actually words on seams, but the seams can tell you a lot as you're sewing. Look for the points where your seams have previously intersected for signs of where the points will be in your block, and sew just to the right of the intersecting seams. If you sew on the left side of that intersection, you'll have missing points. Good luck matching things up!

6. Sew 2½" x 8½" A rectangles to the long sides of each unit from step 5. Press the seam allowances toward the rectangles. Make 30.

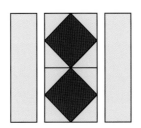
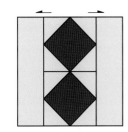

Make 30.

7. Sew half-square-triangle units to both ends of a 2½" x 4½" A rectangle as shown. Press the seam allowances toward the rectangle. Make 60 units.

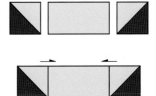

Make 60.

8. Pin and sew two units from step 7 to the top and bottom of a unit from step 6. Press the seam allowances in one direction. Make 30.

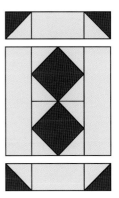

Make 30.

9. Lay out two 5¼" D triangles, four 5¼" A triangles, and one unit from step 2 as shown. Sew D triangles to A triangles and press the seam allowances toward the D triangle. Sew A triangles to the center unit; press the seam allowances toward the center. Then sew the triangle units to the center unit and press the seam allowances toward the D triangles. Make 30.

Make 30.

57

10. Sew 2½" x 4½" D rectangles to the top and bottom of each unit from step 9. Press the seam allowances in one direction. Make 30.

Make 30.

11. Pin and sew one unit from step 8 and one unit from step 10 together as shown to complete a block. Press the seam allowances in one direction. Make 30 blocks.

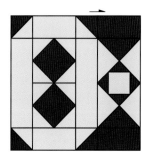

Make 30.

ASSEMBLING THE QUILT TOP

1. Lay out six rows of five blocks each, rotating the blocks as shown in the quilt assembly diagram below. Pin and sew the blocks together in rows, pressing the seam allowances in opposite directions from row to row.

2. Sew the rows together to complete the quilt top. Press the seam allowances in one direction.

Quilt assembly

FINISHING THE QUILT

1. Cut the length of the backing fabric in half to create two 72"-long pieces. Sew the two pieces together side by side and press the seam allowances open.

2. Referring to "Basting a Quilt Sandwich" on page 77, layer the backing, batting, and quilt top; then baste the layers together. Use your favorite quilting technique to quilt a design that you love.

3. Referring to "Binding" on page 78 and using the 2½"-wide strips, bind your quilt.

triangle fury

FINISHED QUILT: 45" x 54"
FINISHED BLOCK: 4½" x 9"

"Triangle Fury" is an edgy little quilt. I opted to paper piece this pattern to keep the crisp edges and points intact. The bold triangles in a variety of sizes are a little quirky and definitely eye-catching. Have fun selecting fabrics and piecing this stunning quilt.

MATERIALS

Yardage is based on 42"-wide fabric.

2½ yards of A fabric (lightest) for blocks
1⅓ yards of D fabric (darkest) for blocks
⅝ yard of B fabric (medium) for blocks
½ yard of fabric for binding
2 yards of fabric for backing*
51" x 60" piece of batting

You'll need 3 yards if you don't want an additional seam in your backing.

CUTTING

From the D fabric, cut:
4 strips, 8¾" x 42"; crosscut into 15 squares, 8¾" x 8¾". Cut the squares into quarters diagonally to yield 60 triangles.
2 strips, 3¾" x 42"; crosscut into 15 squares, 3¾" x 3¾". Cut the squares into quarters diagonally to yield 60 triangles.

From the A fabric, cut:
4 strips, 8" x 42"; crosscut into 60 rectangles, 2¼" x 8"
5 strips, 6" x 42"; crosscut into 30 squares, 6" x 6". Cut the squares in half diagonally to yield 60 triangles.
4 strips, 4½" x 42"; crosscut into 60 rectangles, 2¼" x 4½"

From the B fabric, cut:
3 strips, 6¼" x 42"; crosscut into 15 squares, 6¼" x 6¼". Cut the squares into quarters diagonally to yield 60 triangles.

From the binding fabric, cut:
6 strips, 2½" x 42"

Designed by Amy Ellis; pieced by Mary Kolb; machine quilted by Natalia Bonner

Paper Piecing Tips

1. Shorten your stitch length to 1.5 mm. More perforations make it easy to remove papers.

2. The printed side of the pattern is the reverse of the finished block; make sure all your fabrics are right side up after pressing them over the seam allowances.

3. Hold the paper and the fabric piece up to the light to verify that you have enough seam allowance before stitching.

4. Make an extra copy (or two) of the pattern to practice on before getting started.

5. Depending on how you like to sew, you can repeat the same step for each block or complete one block before starting the next.

6. Begin stitching every seam at least $\frac{1}{4}$" before the seam line and finish $\frac{1}{4}$" beyond the seam line so seams won't rip out when you remove the paper.

7. Starting with the smallest triangle, add pieces in numerical order, trimming any excess fabric as you sew.

PIECING THE BLOCKS

Using a paper foundation pattern will stabilize the bias edges and ensure crisp points in these blocks.

1. Make 60 copies of the foundation pattern on page 63. Trim the pattern to a comfortable size, if desired, leaving at least $\frac{1}{4}$" around the outside cutting line.

2. Place a $3\frac{3}{4}$" D triangle right side up on the blank (unmarked) side of the pattern. Make sure the fabric covers all of area 1 by at least $\frac{1}{4}$" on all sides and pin in place. Lay a

$2\frac{1}{4}$" x $4\frac{1}{2}$" A rectangle on top of the triangle, right sides together, and sew on the line between areas 1 and 2. Flip the rectangle over the seam allowances and press.

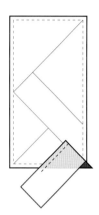

Press.

3. Lay a B triangle on top of the A rectangle, right sides together, and sew on the line between areas 2 and 3. Flip the triangle over the seam allowances and press. Continue in the same way, adding pieces in numerical order until the pattern is completely covered with fabric pieces. Trim the block to measure 5" x $9\frac{1}{2}$", including seam allowances. Make 60 blocks.

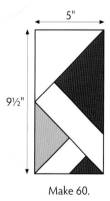

Make 60.

ASSEMBLING THE QUILT TOP

1. Lay out six rows of 10 blocks each, rotating the blocks as shown in the quilt assembly diagram on page 62. Pin and sew the blocks together in rows, pressing the seam allowances in opposite directions from row to row.

2. Sew the rows together to complete the quilt top. Press the seam allowances in one direction.

Quilt assembly

3. Stay stitch ⅛" from the edge of the quilt top to help stabilize any bias-cut edges. Remove the paper foundations from the blocks.

FINISHING THE QUILT

1. Cut the length of the backing fabric into one 42" x 60" piece and two 10" x 42" pieces. Sew the two 10"-wide pieces end to end to make an 84"-long piece; trim the piece to 60" long. Join the two 60"-long pieces side by side and press the seam allowances open.

2. Referring to "Basting a Quilt Sandwich" on page 77, layer the backing, batting, and quilt top; then baste the layers together. Use your favorite quilting technique to quilt a design that you love.

3. Referring to "Binding" on page 78 and using the 2½"-wide strips, bind your quilt.

Bed Quilt Option

Consider making 60 blocks and piecing them between 22" x 90½" and 42" x 90½" pieces of fabric. For a quilt measuring 90½" x 90½", you'll need:

2½ yards of A fabric (lightest) for blocks
1⅓ yards of D fabric (darkest) for blocks
⅝ yard of B fabric (medium) for blocks
5¼ yards of fabric for quilt top and binding
8¼ yards of fabric for backing
96" x 96" piece of batting

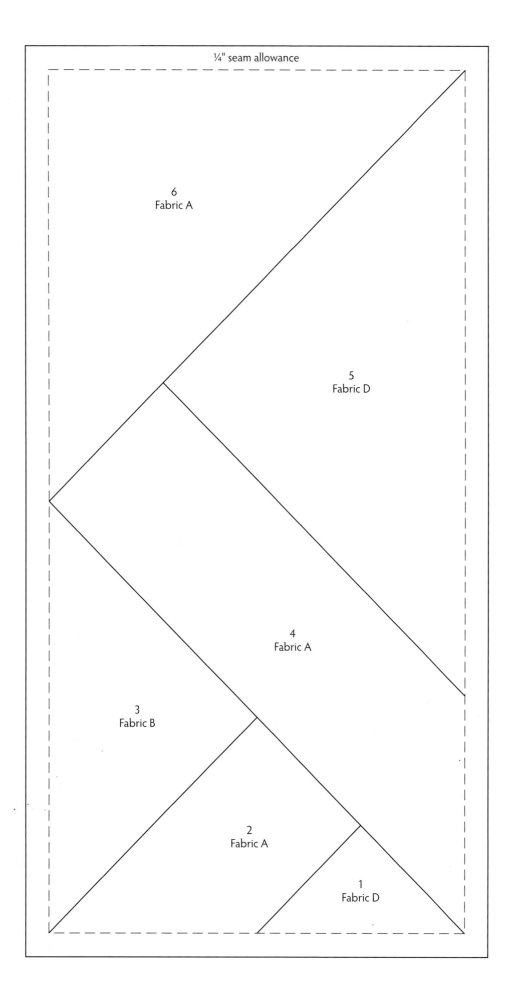

¼" seam allowance

6
Fabric A

5
Fabric D

4
Fabric A

3
Fabric B

2
Fabric A

1
Fabric D

TRIANGLE FURY

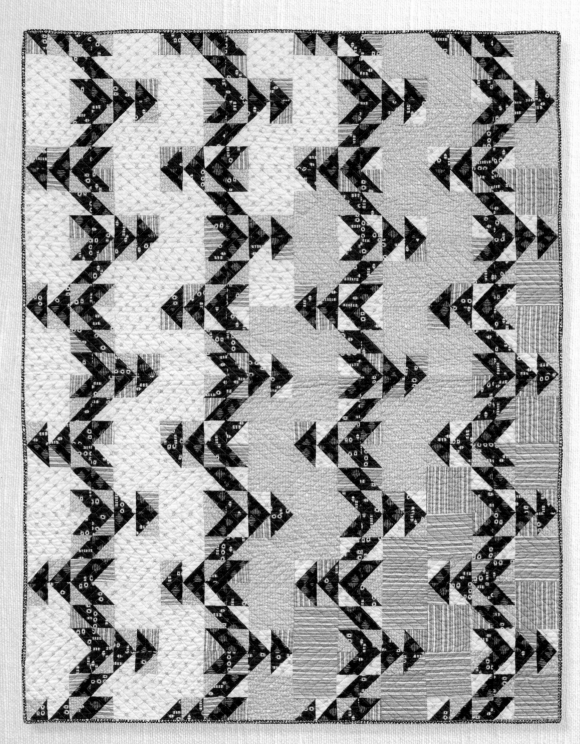

Designed and pieced by Amy Ellis; machine quilted by Natalia Bonner

piked peaks

FINISHED QUILT: 48½" x 60½"
FINISHED BLOCK: 6" x 6"

This controlled-scrappy version of "Piked Peaks" could easily be more planned, with less fabric variety, but sometimes using what you have on hand is fun—and produces gorgeous results. This block can be turned to create any number of quilt designs. Have fun making this quilt your own.

MATERIALS

Yardage is based on 42"-wide fabric.

3 yards *total* of assorted A fabrics (lightest) for blocks
1½ yards *total* of assorted C fabrics (medium) for blocks
½ yard of fabric for binding
3⅛ yards of fabric for backing
54" x 66" piece of batting

Baby Quilt Option

To make 48 blocks for a quilt measuring 36" x 48", you'll need:

1¾ yards *total* of assorted A fabrics (lightest) for blocks
1 yard *total* of assorted C fabrics (medium) for blocks
½ yard of fabric for binding
1½ yards of fabric for backing
42" x 54" piece of batting

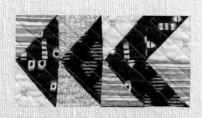

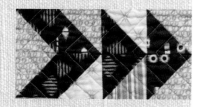

CUTTING

From the assorted A fabrics, cut *a total of:*
10 strips, 4½" x 42"; crosscut into 80 squares, 4½" x 4½"
8 strips, 6" x 42"; crosscut into 50 squares, 6" x 6"*

From the assorted C fabrics, cut *a total of:*
8 strips, 6" x 42"; crosscut into 50 squares, 6" x 6"*

From the binding fabric, cut:
6 strips, 2½" x 42"

*If you're using a GO! cutter, don't cut these pieces. See "Ready, Set, GO!" on page 66 instead.

Ready, Set, GO!

If you have a GO! cutter and the 2"-finished half-square-triangle die, you may choose to assemble the half-square-triangle units from die-cut pieces. Cut 7 strips, 7" wide, from the A and C fabrics in place of the 6"-wide strips in the cutting instructions. Fold each strip into five layers before running it through the GO! cutter, yielding 400 triangles of each color.

PIECING THE BLOCKS

1. To make half-square-triangle units, draw intersecting diagonal lines on the wrong side of each 6" A square. Layer each marked square with a 6" C square, right sides together. Sew ¼" on each side of both drawn lines.

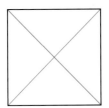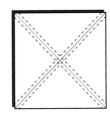

2. Cut the squares apart horizontally and vertically. Then cut the squares on the drawn diagonal lines to make 400 half-square-triangle units. Press the seam allowances and trim the units to measure 2½" square.

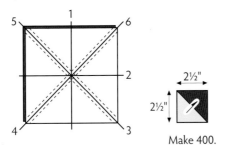

2½"

2½"

Make 400.

3. Sew two half-square-triangle units together as shown. Press the seam allowances in the direction indicated. Make 80 units.

Make 80.

4. Sew three half-square-triangle units together as shown. Press the seam allowances in the direction indicated. Make 80 units.

Make 80.

5. Pin and sew a unit from step 3 to the top of each 4½" A square. On half of the units, press the seam allowances toward the square. On the remaining units, press the seam allowances away from the square. Make 80.

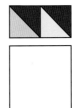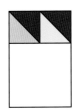

Make 80.

66

6. Pin and sew the units from step 4 to the units from step 5 as shown to complete the block. Press the seam allowances toward the square. Make 80 blocks.

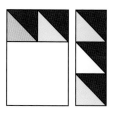 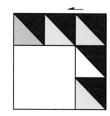

Make 80.

ASSEMBLING THE QUILT TOP

1. Lay out 10 rows of eight blocks each, rotating the blocks as shown in the quilt assembly diagram below, or in any arrangement you like. There are numerous layout options for these blocks. Pin and sew the blocks together in rows, pressing the seam allowances in opposite directions from row to row.

2. Pin and sew the rows together to complete the quilt top. Press the seam allowances in one direction.

FINISHING THE QUILT

1. Cut the length of the backing fabric in half to create two 54"-long pieces. Sew the two pieces together side by side and press the seam allowances open.

2. Referring to "Basting a Quilt Sandwich" on page 77, layer the backing, batting, and quilt top; then baste the layers together. Use your favorite quilting technique to quilt a design that you love.

3. Referring to "Binding" on page 78 and using the 2½"-wide strips, bind your quilt.

Quilt assembly

Designed by Amy Ellis; pieced by Kendra Nitta; machine quilted by Natalia Bonner

shifting sands

FINISHED QUILT: 50½" x 60½"
FINISHED BLOCK: 10" x 10"

The Log Cabin blocks of "Shifting Sands" are so versatile! This simple quilt can be customized to your space and sewn in an afternoon. Consider adding a subtle pop of color to the block centers for a "wow" moment in your quilt.

MATERIALS

Yardage is based on 42"-wide fabric.

⅞ yard *each* of B1 and B2 fabrics (medium) for blocks

⅝ yard *each* of C1 and C2 fabrics (medium) for blocks

⅓ yard *each* of 2 A fabrics (lightest) for blocks

½ yard of C3 fabric (medium) for blocks

½ yard of fabric for binding

3¼ yards of fabric for backing

56" x 66" piece of batting

CUTTING

From the C3 fabric, cut:
4 strips, 3" x 42"; crosscut into:
    15 rectangles, 3" x 4"
    15 rectangles, 3" x 6½"

From *each* of the A fabrics, cut:
2 strips, 4" x 42"; crosscut into 15 squares,
    4" x 4" (30 total)

From the B1 fabric, cut:
1 strip, 10½" x 42"; crosscut into 8 rectangles,
    4½" x 10½"
1 strip, 6½" x 42"; crosscut into 8 rectangles,
    4½" x 6½"
3 strips, 3" x 42"; crosscut into:
    8 rectangles, 3" x 4"
    8 rectangles, 3" x 6½"

Continued on page 70

From the B2 fabric, cut:

1 strip, 10½" x 42"; crosscut into 7 rectangles, 4½" x 10½"

1 strip, 6½" x 42"; crosscut into 7 rectangles, 4½" x 6½"

2 strips, 3" x 42"; crosscut into:
  7 rectangles, 3" x 4"
  7 rectangles, 3" x 6½"

From the C1 fabric, cut:

1 strip, 10½" x 42"; crosscut into 8 rectangles, 4½" x 10½"

1 strip, 6½" x 42"; crosscut into 8 rectangles, 4½" x 6½"

From the C2 fabric, cut:

1 strip, 10½" x 42"; crosscut into 7 rectangles, 4½" x 10½"

1 strip, 6½" x 42"; crosscut into 7 rectangles, 4½" x 6½"

From the binding fabric, cut:

6 strips, 2½" x 42"

PIECING THE BLOCKS

These simple Log Cabin blocks are fun to make and the results are different every time. Before you begin, decide which A square to use with each set of B and C rectangles. I used four different color combinations for my blocks. Press the seam allowances away from the center as you work.

1. Sew a 3" x 4" C3 rectangle to the bottom of a 4" A square and press. Sew a 3" x 6½" C3 rectangle to the right side of the square; press. Make eight.

Make 8.

2. Sew a 4½" x 6½" B1 rectangle to the top of the unit from step 1; press. Sew a 4½" x 10½" B1 rectangle to the left side of the unit to complete the block; press. Make eight blocks.

 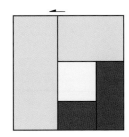

Make 8.

3. Repeat steps 1 and 2, using the remaining C3 rectangles, the 4½" x 6½" and 4½" x 10½" B2 rectangles, and seven A squares to make seven blocks.

Make 7.

4. Repeat steps 1 and 2, using the 3" x 4" and 3" x 6½" B1 rectangles, the C1 rectangles, and eight A squares to make eight blocks.

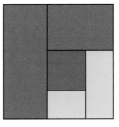

Make 8.

5. Repeat steps 1 and 2, using the 3" x 4" and 3" x 6½" B2 rectangles, the C2 rectangles, and the remaining A squares to make seven blocks.

Make 7.

ASSEMBLING THE QUILT TOP

1. Lay out six rows of five blocks each, rotating the blocks as shown below. Pin and sew the blocks together in rows, pressing the seam allowances in opposite directions from row to row.

2. Pin and sew the rows together to complete the quilt top. Press the seam allowances in one direction.

FINISHING THE QUILT

1. Cut the length of the backing fabric in half to create two 56"-long pieces. Sew the two pieces together side by side and press the seam allowances open.

2. Referring to "Basting a Quilt Sandwich" on page 77, layer the backing, batting, and quilt top; then baste the layers together. Use your favorite quilting technique to quilt a design that you love.

3. Referring to "Binding" on page 78 and using the 2½"-wide strips, bind your quilt.

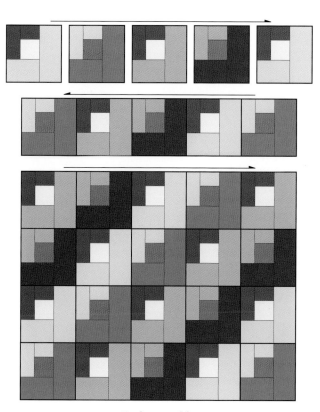

Quilt assembly

quiltmaking basics

The following pages outline the basics for making a quilt. I've included helpful tips for new quilters as well as those who want a refresher. If you need more details about any part of the process, please visit AmysCreativeSide.com or ShopMartingale.com/HowtoQuilt.

TOOLS

A wide range of tools and gadgets are available for quilters. Here's a list of the most basic necessities to make the quilts in this book.

Sewing machine. My first quilts were made with a small sewing machine that had just nine stitch options. If you need to purchase a machine, you don't have to break the bank—though if you're absolutely certain this will be a lifelong venture into quilting, a machine can be a good investment.

Rotary cutter. The first tool to purchase for rotary cutting is this "pizza cutter" for fabric, which is super sharp and makes cutting precise pieces easy. A 60 mm cutter is best for straight cuts through many fabric layers, while a 28 mm model pivots easily around curves. Many quilters find a 45 mm cutter to be a great all-purpose size. Find the one that's most comfortable for you.

Two rotary-cutter options

Self-healing mat. A special mat for rotary cutting is essential to protect surfaces and keep cutting blades in good shape. This is one tool that needs to be large; an 18" x 24" mat is a good size for cutting full-width strips.

Rulers. There are countless acrylic rulers in different sizes and shapes to make rotary cutting precise and fast. My favorite rulers are a 6½" x 24" for cutting strips and rectangles, a 6" square for cutting smaller pieces, and a 12½" square for trimming blocks after they've been sewn together. Other sizes and shapes are handy, but they're not necessary to make the quilts in this book.

Water-soluble pen. There are a variety of marking tools available for fabric, but I tend to use this inexpensive option, available from fabric retailers. Any tool used must glide across the fabric smoothly, without pulling, as you mark.

Sewing-machine needles. I use size 80/12 universal needles for piecing and a slightly smaller 75/11 for machine quilting.

Sharpen Your Ears

If you ever actually hear the needle hitting the fabric, it's time to change your needle. It makes a "ping" sound when dull.

Thread. A general rule of thumb in quiltmaking is that the fabric and thread fiber content should be the same; when using 100% cotton fabrics, use 100% cotton thread. However, cotton thread isn't always available and its colors may be limited, so use your discretion as needed. I prefer 50-weight thread for piecing my quilts. The bigger the number the finer the thread, meaning less bulk is added to seams. It's the opposite with sewing-machine needles, where a larger number means a larger needle.

Straight pins. I like to pin pieces together before sewing. My favorite pins are 1" to 1½" long with round, glass heads. They're easy to hold onto when pinning.

Safety pins. Look for a large packet of safety pins available at fabric stores; they're used to baste the layers of the quilt together prior to quilting, so you'll need many.

Hand-quilting thread. I prefer this stiffer, heartier thread for hand stitching bindings in place. Having both warm and cool neutral colors around for just this purpose is very helpful.

FABRIC

When selecting fabrics it's important first and foremost to love the color and/or print—even for neutrals! Keep this in mind as you browse fabric options; when you've found one fabric that you love, find others that work with it. Balancing color, print, and value can take time to learn, although some are blessed with a designer's eye. Step back and look at your fabric selections side by side to get a little perspective. Take cues from the fabrics used in my projects, and find the fabrics that you love to make your project special and unique.

You can buy yardage, fat quarters, or precut fabrics (see "Words for the Wise" at right) to make the quilts in this book, or you can use a combination of the above. Treat all the fabrics in one quilt in the same manner.

I don't prewash my fabric, but you may if you like. Always take the time to press fabrics before cutting, however. I suggest using spray starch for a nice crisp finish to the fabric, and find that there's less stretching of the grain after spray starch is applied. When pressing, be careful not to distort the grain; instead of sliding the iron, lift and press as needed (see "Pressing" on page 76).

Using fabrics you love is a must!

Words for the Wise

Fat quarter. A quilting staple, this small cut of fabric measures 18" x 21" and offers more cutting flexibility than a traditional ¼-yard cut.

Selvage. This manufacturer-finished fabric edge typically includes identifiers for the fabric manufacturer. I've seen them saved and used in great selvage-only projects.

Length of fabric. This is the yardage that you purchased. Typically, strips are cut across the fabric width, but occasionally borders are cut from the length of the fabric.

Width of fabric. This is the selvage-to-selvage width of the fabric. Most quilting cottons are 42" to 45" wide, while decorator fabrics are 54" to 60" wide.

73

CUTTING

Always be careful using your rotary cutter—it's a round razor blade! Many quilters (me included) have scars on their fingers from incautious moments. Always keep the blade guard or safety on when the cutter is not in use, and keep your fingers away from the ruler edge when cutting.

If you have young children or curious animals, take care to keep your rotary cutter out of their reach at all times.

Using a rotary cutter becomes easier with practice. Always apply firm pressure when cutting to ensure a straight cut through all the layers. Cut as many strips as possible with the width of your cutting mat, and then reposition the fabric.

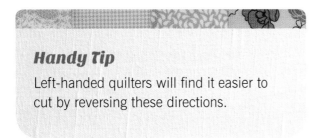

Handy Tip

Left-handed quilters will find it easier to cut by reversing these directions.

Cutting Strips and Segments

Cutting strips, and then cutting segments from the strips, is quick and easy. Verify the required width and measure twice before cutting—you don't want to miscut your beautiful fabrics.

1. To cut strips, align the required measurement on the ruler with the straightened fabric edge. For example, to cut a 2"-wide strip, place the 2" mark of the ruler on the edge of the fabric.

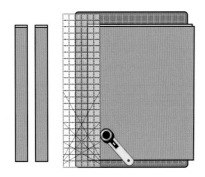

2. To crosscut squares and rectangles, begin with strips in the required width. Use a ruler and rotary cutter to remove the selvages from the strips. Align the required measurement on the ruler with the left edge of the strip and cut a square or a rectangle. Continue cutting until you have the required number of pieces.

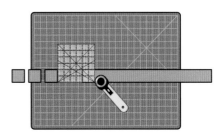

3. Cutting segments from strip sets is a speedy method used in some quilts. When cutting these segments, use a seam between strips as your guide instead of the top or bottom raw edge. This often means making the initial cut slightly wider than specified, and then rotating the segment to clean up the segment's other edge as well. Don't worry about wasting fabric—extra fabric has been allowed in the materials.

First, trim the ends of the strip set to square it up. Second, align the required measurement on the ruler with the left edge of the strip set, and align a horizontal line on the ruler with a seam in the strip set. Cut the required number of segments.

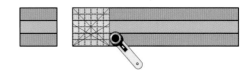

PIECING

I am not a perfectionist. I do aim as close to perfection as possible, but I've learned that perfection comes at too high a price. The process of making a quilt is enjoyable if you allow yourself to enjoy it. If you do make a mistake, learn from it and move on. Don't point it out, and no one else will notice. And each quilt will be better than the last!

Sewing an Accurate ¼" Seam Allowance

Perfecting your ¼" seam allowance will make quilting easier. If a ¼" foot is available for your sewing machine, great!

A ¼" foot for sewing machine

If you don't have a ¼" foot, don't despair. Using tape or a permanent marker, mark the machine's soleplate ¼" from the standard needle position. To quickly test for an accurate ¼" seam allowance, cut two 2½" squares and sew them together on one side. Press the seam allowances as you usually do—to one side or open. Measure the unit. It should measure *exactly* 4½".

If your unit doesn't measure 4½", consider moving the needle to the right or left one or two positions or moving your mark slightly. If you change the needle position, be certain that the presser foot can accommodate the shift to avoid breaking a needle. Work through the test again to verify that you have perfected your ¼" seam allowance.

Using Pins

I like to pin pieces together en masse to make a large stack of seams to sew. I can be certain that my edges are aligned and ready to sew without having to stop and double-check each one. This makes my time more efficient when I'm able to sit and sew. See "Chain Piecing" on page 76.

Pinning your pieces in place before stitching is imperative to achieve accurate points and match seam junctions. Place the pieces right sides together, and then slightly separate the edges you're preparing to sew. Visually verify that the seams match, and then pin.

When matching seams, pin on both sides of the existing seam, perpendicular to the seam being sewn. Using one pin on each side makes a good reminder for me to slow down and take the pin out just as I am about to sew over it.

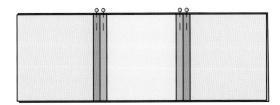

Safe Sewing

Don't sew over pins. You may break a needle, which can send the tip flying or even damage your machine. Stay safe.

When joining rows, always match seams first, and then the row ends; finish by pinning the middle of the rows as needed. When matching seams and joining rows, there may be a touch of excess fabric on one side. It happens—thankfully fabric is very forgiving. It's possible to ease the excess into the seam while pinning by spreading the excess out as much as possible. Work slowly over the seam while sewing, with the longer side against the feed dogs when possible.

If the seams don't match as well as you'd like after sewing, take out the portion that's mis-aligned; then turn the work over, repin, and sew from the other side.

Using a Seam Ripper

When you need to take out a seam or two (it happens to all of us), slide your seam ripper under the stitches on the fabric wrong side, cutting the thread every few stitches. Turn the work over and gently tug the thread free.

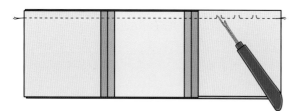

If you're removing just a small segment from a long seam, you'll need to clip the thread on either end of the segment prior to removing the stitches and resewing the seam.

Chain Piecing

When I have a stack of pinned pieces ready to sew, I like to piece them one after the other, without stopping to snip the thread. I use less thread and don't have to hold the threads to start a seam with each unit sewn. Chain piecing in this manner is a big time-saver.

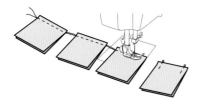

Pressing

Gentle pressing is an essential step in sewing a quilt top that lies flat. Pressing differs from ironing in that you lift the iron and set it down in one place instead of sliding it over the fabric. In the projects, I've indicated the direction for pressing the seam allowances.

Setting seams prior to pressing helps reduce stretching and movement in your seams. To set, press each seam just as you have sewn it, before opening and separating the fabrics.

To press the seam allowances to one side, lay the sewn strip set on the ironing board, with the fabric you are pressing toward on top. Press the seam flat to set it. Use the edge of the iron to open the fabrics and turn the upper layer over the seam allowances. Be careful not to stretch the pieces out of shape as you press.

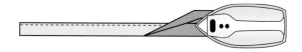

Trimming Your Blocks

When you've finished piecing your blocks, take a few moments to trim them to the exact size; straightening the edges makes assembling the quilt top simpler. This is why I love my 12½" square ruler!

Place the 12½" square ruler on top of the block, centering the block by aligning the ruler markings with some of the seam lines in the block. Trim two edges of the block. Rotate the block and trim the other two edges.

BASTING A QUILT SANDWICH

There are a few different ways to baste a quilt, but the most efficient (and budget friendly) is on the floor with safety pins. You can use the pins over and over, and they hold the quilt securely, no matter how much you wrestle with your quilt while quilting.

Backing Measurements

I've given instructions and specified adequate yardage for making a backing 6" larger than the quilt top, which means an extra 3" on each side. This is plenty if you're going to be doing the quilting yourself. If you hire a long-arm quilter, check with her to see how much larger she wants the backing and buy additional yardage if necessary.

1. Prepare your backing fabric, pressing out all the creases and wrinkles.

2. Lay the quilt backing on the floor, right side down. Use masking tape to secure the edges to the floor. Pull the fabric taut without stretching it. Avoid taping the corners, which may stretch the grain out of square.

3. Lay the batting on the backing. Smooth out wrinkles with your hands (or a cool iron for stubborn creases), working from the center outward.

4. Add the quilt top, right side up. Straighten and smooth.

5. Begin pinning with safety pins near the center and smooth out any excess fabric as you work your way toward the quilt edges. Add a pin every 5" to 7" (a hand length), until the sandwich is completely basted. Remove the tape and get ready to quilt!

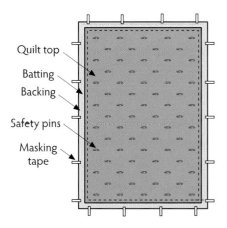

MACHINE QUILTING

Quilting with a standard sewing machine is possible! Check your machine booklet for any instructions specific to your machine. Quilting can be a challenge, depending on the project size, but watching the texture work into the quilt is so rewarding.

If you haven't done any machine quilting yet, I recommend starting with a walking foot. The walking foot feeds the quilt layers evenly as you guide them under the needle. Obviously a walking foot works in straight lines, but you can also create textured waves of quilting with slight movement. Some decorative stitches can be used for quilting; don't limit yourself or your machine, but do test stitch first on fabric scraps.

A darning or free-motion foot allows you to stitch designs by moving the quilt sandwich in any direction. Practice the pattern on paper to determine how to move the fabric under the needle. When you're ready, put together a small quilt sandwich, about 18" square, and see how your machine responds.

Check your machine manual for specific free-motion settings. You may need to shorten the stitch length to 0 and cover or lower the feed dogs, removing the machine's ability to feed the fabric and giving you complete control.

When free-motion quilting, it's best to start quilting on one side and slowly work your way to the left or right, depending on what's most comfortable to you. Turning your machine 90°, so the needle is close to you, offers more space to move the fabric under the needle. Try it!

After you've quilted your quilt, trim the batting and excess backing even with the quilt-top edges and make sure it's square. Squaring a quilt may require a little muscle; giving a little tug to your quilt prior to trimming is acceptable.

BINDING

When I was learning to quilt with books like this, the binding was the one piece of the quilt I could not visualize. I did it all sorts of ways, until it finally clicked for me. I hope that I explain it here so that you understand from the start.

Preparing the Binding

Cut binding strips as instructed for each quilt project.

1. With right sides together, lay one strip over the other at a 90° angle. Let the selvage end of each strip extend beyond the raw edge of the other. Mark the diagonal where the strips overlap, pin, and sew on the marked line.

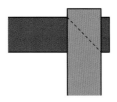

2. Trim the excess fabric ¼" outside the seam and press the seam allowances open. Repeat to join all the strips.

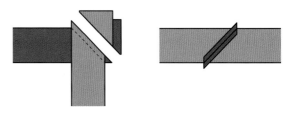

3. Fold the binding in half with wrong sides together and press to make a 1¼"-wide strip with a folded edge on one side and raw edges on the other.

Attaching the Binding

I use a walking foot to attach the binding; it's a great tool for controlling four layers of fabric and one layer of batting. Pin before stitching if desired, but I've found that if I take my time sewing the binding around the quilt, pinning isn't usually necessary.

1. Align the raw edges of the quilt and binding. Leaving a 10" to 12" tail, begin sewing in the middle of one quilt edge using a ¼" seam allowance. When you arrive at a corner, stop sewing ¼" from the approaching edge to miter the binding. Backstitch, remove the quilt from the sewing machine, and clip the thread.

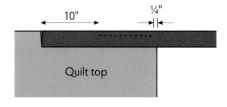

2. Turn the quilt to stitch the next side. Fold the binding upward, away from the quilt, and then fold the binding back down onto itself. Keeping the raw edges aligned with the edge of the quilt top, stitch the next edge.

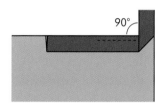

3. Continue around the quilt in the same manner until you're 18" from the beginning stitches. Remove the quilt from the sewing machine to join the binding tails. Lay the binding end on top of the beginning tail. Mark the end to indicate a 2½" overlap and cut the excess.

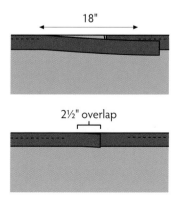

18"

2½" overlap

4. Unfold both binding tails and lay them on top of each other at a 90° angle, with right sides together. Pin to keep the ends in place.

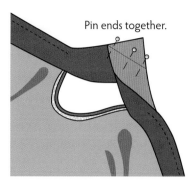

Pin ends together.

5. Mark a diagonal line across the overlap and sew on the line. Check to make sure the binding fits the edge of the quilt and adjust if necessary; when the fit is correct, trim the excess binding ¼" from the seam line and press the seam open. Refold and finish sewing the binding to the quilt.

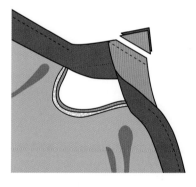

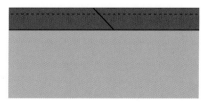

79

6. Press the binding away from the quilt top for easier handling when folding the binding over the quilt edges. Blindstitch the binding to the quilt backing, staying away from the corners and with the binding's folded edge just covering the seam line. A miter will form at each corner; blindstitch the miters in place.

QUILTMAKING BASICS

Acknowledgments

I've made many friends who have contributed to the creation of this book. I'd like to specifically thank:

Amy, April, Audrie, Karen, Kendra, Mary, Sherri, and Trish, whose help was invaluable in piecing some of the projects included in this book.

Natalia Bonner of Piece N Quilt for the beautiful machine quilting on all of the quilts.

Baby Lock for the fantastic Melody sewing machine used to piece many of the quilts and all of my sewing projects.

AdornIt, Andover Fabrics, Cloud 9 Fabrics, Dear Stella Fabrics, Moda Fabrics, Riley Blake Fabrics, Robert Kaufman Fabrics, and Windham Fabrics for the gorgeous fabrics included in this book.

The Warm Company for the fabulous Warm & Natural batting in each of the quilts.

Lapel Stick for the excellent product used in piecing some of the projects.

about the author

AMY ELLIS has always loved fabric, and the creative process of designing with it. She's called herself a quilter for the last 12 years, and has been sewing since the age of 10. You can often find her drafting a new quilt pattern and experimenting with fabrics until it's just right. Quilting is her creative therapy in the midst of a busy household, and she loves to inspire new quilters to find their own way.

Since diving into the online community in 2008, Amy has authored three books and her quilts have been included in many collaborative book projects. Her patterns and articles have been published in several prominent magazines. See what Amy has been working on lately by visiting her website at AmysCreativeSide.com.